心はずむ毎日の、うれしい食習慣

GOOD HABIT

GOOD life from happy eating **HABIT**

村田英理子

山川出版社

CONTENTS

CHAPTER 1

MAKING A BASE

ベースメイク

CHAPTER 2

POWER UP

パワーアップ

* 計量単位は、大さじ1＝15ml、小さじ1＝5mlです。
* 電子レンジやオーブンは機種により、加熱具合に多少の差が出ることがあります。様子を見ながら調節してください。
* 食材を洗う、野菜の皮をむく、ヘタや種を取るなど、基本的な下ごしらえは作り方から省いています。適宜行ってください。

本書に掲載されている内容は2020年10月現在のものです。

CHAPTER 3

POWER CHARGE

パワーチャージ

CHAPTER 4

CHILL OUT

チルアウト

GOOD HABIT PEOPLE

はじめに

「GOOD HABIT」。聞き慣れない言葉かもしれませんが、読み方はグッドハビット、英語で「良い習慣」という意味です。食事は習慣だと考える私が、ずっと続けていきたいシンプルな良い食習慣と、アスリートフードが真ん中にあるくらしがこの一冊に詰まっています。

アスリートのための食事と聞くとストイックでつらいものをイメージされるかもしれません。ですが食事は、毎日3回もあるイベント。無理をすると長続きしません。私も数々の失敗を経験しながら、「シンプルに、細く長く続けていくこと」の大切さに気づき、自分らしいGOOD HABITにたどり着きました。それは、プロラグビープレーヤーである夫との結婚を機に学んだスポーツ栄養の理論と、日々の食事サポートの経験をかけ合わせてできた、3つのマイルール。ルールといっても難しいことはなく、ご家庭で食べなじみのある料理に、少し足したり引いたりするだけで、ストレスなくバランスの良い食事になるアイデアです。

さて、夫のために作ってきたはずの食事でしたが、同じものを食べるようになってから、何よりも自分自身の体に変化が起きていることに気づきました。息子を出産するまでは、3時間の通勤をしながら、海外営業の仕事をし、限られた時間と体力でプロアスリート向けの食事を作り…というなかなかハードな生活でしたが、慢性的にあったむくみや疲労感は激減し、体重の変動もなくなり、肌の調子も絶好調。少しばかり暴飲暴食する日があっても、ブレない良い状態を保てるようになったのです。そして、妊娠中には息子にも十分栄養が行き届いていたのでしょうか、4,315gの特大ビッグベイビーが産まれました。そう、アスリートのための食事って、実は私のような一般人にも良い食事なのです。

これから、村田家で実践してきた「GOOD HABIT 良い食習慣」の軸となる3つのルールとレシピ、そして第一線で活躍されているトップアスリートとそのご家族が、どんな考えをもってGOOD HABITを実践しているのか、特別レシピを添えてたっぷりお伝えしていきます。

みなさんの食事を作る時間がちょっと楽しくなった！これなら続けられそう！と思うきっかけになればと願っています。

村田英理子

INTRODUCTION

"Good habits." Although it can seem overwhelming, that's what diet and nutrition is really all about.
As someone whose private and professional life centers around the nutritional needs of pro athletes, I've put together this book to help others to cultivate and maintain these kinds of healthy dietary habits. I call this my "GOOD HABIT" philosophy.

When you hear terms like "athletic nutrition," it may conjure up images of hardcore, restrictive diets that need to be endured, rather than enjoyed. But meals are a part of life that we experience multiple times every day, and if you make every meal unenjoyable you're not likely to continue very long. After lots of trial and error, I've found that the most effective plan for a better diet is to develop your own slate of GOOD HABITs; simple, healthy choices that you can commit to consistently. For me, after years of marriage to a professional rugby player and my own research into sports nutrition, I've been able to come up with three rules for a healthy diet. Don't worry when you read the word "rules." These are just guidelines for simple things to adjust in your cooking to achieve better nutrition for your whole family, without unnecessary stress.

As I ate meal after meal of the cooking that I had optimized for my husband's performance, I began to notice changes in my own body as well. Before my son was born, I fought through the hard daily schedule of a three hour commute, an international sales job, as well as the challenge of maintaining my husband's diet, and keeping our household running. But even amidst all that stress, as I ate what he ate I found that my tiredness and swelling had decreased, I could avoid wild weight fluctuations, and my skin was in great condition. Even better, I could keep all of these benefits even if I took the occasional day off of my scheduled eating. During pregnancy, the nutrients must have found their way to my son as well, who was born at the impressive weight of 4,315 grams. The meals I had put together for my athlete husband were helping a normal person like me as well.

In this book, you'll find the Murata family's dietary GOOD HABITs, all guided by my three rules. There are also plenty of easy, nutritious recipes, eaten and enjoyed every day by the family of a high-level professional athlete. I hope that this book will be the start of many people's discovery of healthy cooking that they can enjoy, and leave you thinking, "I can do this!"

ERIKO MURATA

THE GOOD HABIT PHILOSOPHY

GOOD HABITについて

ムダなくムラなく

栄養学を知れば知るほど、栄養素の名前がたくさん出てきます。ビタミンはアルファベットで区別され、さらにビタミンB群の中でB_1やB_6、B_{12}などに細分化されます。ただ、せっかく栄養素の名前を覚えたとしても、あわただしい日常生活の中で活かすチャンスは少ないのが正直なところ。それなら、自分の目で食材を見て、選べる力をつけた方がよほど実践的だと思いませんか。限られた時間の中で、莫大な情報を取捨選択しながら、私がたどり着いたルールが次の3つです。

1. **たんぱく源は2種類以上入れること**
2. **野菜は色の濃いものをとること**
3. **「まごわやさしい」で答え合わせをすること**

3つのルールのベースには、吸収率が良くなる食べ合わせと、栄養バランスアップの仕組みが隠されています。ムラなく食べ合わせることで、口に入れた栄養素をムダなく体に取り入れることができるのです。

レシピの基本となる考え方ですので、もう少し補足しましょう。

1. たんぱく源は2種類以上入れること…「アミノ酸スコア」[※1]を意識したたんぱく質をとる工夫
アミノ酸は20種類ありますが、そのうち必須アミノ酸と呼ばれる9種類は、1つでも不足しているものがあると、そこが吸収量の足切りとなって、桶から水があふれ出るように、それだけのたんぱく質しか生成できずにムダになってしまうのです(アミノ酸の桶の理論)。それを防ぐために、2種類以上のたんぱく源を組み合わせることで、アミノ酸をムラなくとりましょう。

2. 野菜は色の濃いものをとること
野菜には大きく分けて、切っても中まで色が濃い緑黄色野菜と、切ると中の色が薄い淡色野菜があります。栄養素の吸収率を高めるのに必要なビタミン類・ミネラル類が比較的多くふくまれるのは、緑黄色野菜です。できるだけ多くの緑黄色野菜をとる心がけを持ちましょう。

3.「まごわやさしい」で答え合わせ
「まごわやさしい」[※2]とは、7品目の食材を取り入れることで健康的な食生活が送れるという、和食に古くから伝わる合言葉です。食事の準備を進めながらこの合言葉を唱えて、足りなければその食材をさっと足す——答え合わせをして効率よく、栄養バランスをアップさせていきましょう。

※1 アミノ酸の中には、体内で生成することのできない必須アミノ酸と呼ばれるものが9種類あり、それぞれに摂取必要量が定められています。その必要量に対して、食品にふくまれる必須アミノ酸がどれほど満たされているかでアミノ酸スコアは算出されます。100に近い数値であるほど理想的とされています。

※2 「まごわやさしい」は、「豆、ごま(種子類)、わかめ(海藻類)、野菜(野菜を1日350g)、魚(魚介類)、しいたけ(きのこ類)、いも(いも類)」の頭文字。

はじめにお伝えする3つのルールは、毎食心がけたい基本です。アスリートには、トレーニング量の多い日・少ない日、シーズン中、シーズンオフなど、さまざまなシチュエーションがありますが、これらを一年中意識し続けることでいつしか習慣になります。

The three rules I share with you can be used as guidelines for all your meals. An athlete's lifestyle is constantly shifting between heavy and light training, and the on and off-seasons, but these rules can help provide a solid foundation year round, no matter what stage of training you find yourself in.

EVEN AND EFFICIENT

As you dive into nutritional science you'll discover a neverending list of nutrient names. Vitamins come in A, B and other alphabet categories, and each of those can be further divided into B1, B6, B12 etc. But the truth is, even if you manage to memorize all these letters and numbers, it can still be difficult to properly use this knowledge in your busy day-to-day life. That's why, rather than memorizing a long list of necessary vitamins and minerals, it's much more useful to develop your own ability to choose healthy ingredients by simply looking at them with your own two eyes. Because your time is so precious, I've taken the liberty of distilling down all of these complicated nutritional theory into three simple rules:

1. Include at least two types of protein
2. Focus on richly colored vegetables
3. Include options from the "Big 7" ingredients

These three rules are the secret to achieving greater nutritional balance and nutrient absorption in all of your daily meals. By balancing your diet based on these rules, you can be sure that your body is getting the most out of every bit of food you put into it, helping it to function more cleanly and efficiently.
These rules are the basis for all of my recipes, so let's look at them in a bit more detail:

1. Include at least two types of protein...choosing proteins while keeping in mind their "Amino Score" *1
Among the twenty types of amino acids (the building blocks of protein), there are nine variations that are considered "Essential Amino Acids." Insufficient intake of any of these nine amino acids will limit the amount of nutrients that your body can absorb. Like a barrel of water missing one of it's composite planks, the nutrients you would have taken in instead "spill out," and pass through your body unabsorbed (we call this framing of amino intake the "Barrel Theory of Amino Acids"). To avoid this, we'll focus on taking in at least two different types of proteins with every meal, which will help to fill in any gaps in our amino acid "barrel" and help you get the most out of your nutrition.

2. Focus on richly colored vegetables
Vegetables can be roughly divided into two categories: those that have a deep color throughout even when you cut into them, and those that have a lighter coloration inside. In particular, green and yellow vegetables have an abundance of the vitamins and minerals your body needs to absorb and process nutrients, so when in doubt, aim to include those colors in your cooking.

3. Combine options from the "Big 7" ingredients
The "Big 7" *2 are seven ingredients that have been considered foundational to healthy eating in Japan for generations. Keeping these seven ingredients in mind while you prepare meals will help you to easily add balanced nutrition to any arrangement.

---

*1 The nine essential amino acids cannot be produced by the body, meaning they must be consumed in set amounts through food. A food's "Amino Score" indicates how well it satisfies the requirements for each of these nine essential aminos. The closer the score is to 100, the more of your protein requirements that food fulfills.

*2 The Big 7 are comprised of beans, sesame (and other seeds), seaweed, vegetables (at least 350 grams/day), fish and seafood, mushrooms, and potatoes (or other root vegetables)

MAKING A BASE

ベースメイク

何を目指すにしても結局のところ、体の土台がしっかり整っていることが大切です。口にした食べものを消化吸収でき、栄養素を体のすみずみまで届けられ、不要なものは出すことができる。当たりまえのようですが、案外むずかしいもの。ベースメイクでは、体じゅうにくまなく大切なものを運ぶ役割を持つ「鉄分」と、スムーズに運ぶ手助けをする「良質な脂質」に特に意識を向けています。

鉄分

栄養素や代謝産物を体じゅうに運ぶなどの役割もありますが、私が最も大切だと考えている働きは、体じゅうに酸素を届けることです。この鉄分が不足すると、赤血球（ヘモグロビン）の数が少なくなる結果、酸素が行き渡らなくなり、あちこちで酸欠状態を起こし、いたるところで不調が出ます。

症状例）
脳の酸欠：めまい、立ちくらみ、失神
心臓の酸欠：息切れ、動悸、胸痛
筋肉の酸欠：だるい、疲れやすい、肩こり
末端の酸欠：冷え

実はアスリートに多いのが「隠れ貧血」です。アスリートは、酸素を必要とする筋肉が多いため、鉄の必要量も増えて鉄欠乏になりやすいことや、大量の汗をかくことで鉄分を失いやすいこと、また、走るだけでも、足の裏へのくり返される衝撃により血管内の赤血球が壊れてしまいます。成長期で鉄分必要量が増える子どもや、月経によって鉄分消費量・必要量が増える女性も、貧血のリスクは高まると知られていますが、男性も要注意です。

良質な脂質

食事に気をつかっていても、栄養素を体じゅうに届けてくれるはずの血液がドロドロだったり、血管や細胞が硬いと、体のすみずみまで行き渡らせることができません。そこで注目したいのが、血管を強くしなやかにし、血液をサラサラにする効果が期待できる良質な脂質。ここでは、主に魚に多くふくまれるEPAやDHAといったオメガ３系の脂肪酸をさします。

ともすれば悪いイメージの強い脂質も、持続的なアスリート生活にとって大切な栄養素。「脂質の良質化」という考え方で味方につけていきましょう。まずは、揚げものや脂肪の多いお肉の部位は避け、かわりにオメガ３系の脂肪酸をはじめとした良質な脂質を選んでみる。これだけで、量がそれほど変わらなくても、質が改善され、コンディションの底上げにつながります。

レシピは、次の3つのテーマでお届けしていきます。目的や体調に合わせた食材選び、ふくまれる栄養素の吸収率を高める食べ合わせ、そしてできる限り栄養をムダにしない調理法。このようなちょっとした工夫を楽しみながら食卓を作っていきます。

The recipes that follow can roughly be divided into three basic themes: Choosing the right ingredients for your goals and current condition, eating to maximize your nutrient absorption, and cooking methods to maximize nutrition. Keeping these themes in mind, we can bring a little bit more nutrition to our dinner table, while still enjoying all of our meals.

No matter what goal you're aiming for, the first and most important step is building a solid foundation for your body. We often think of nutrition simply; your body breaks down all the food you eat, extracts the nutrients it needs, and expels everything it doesn't have a use for. But the truth is, achieving this kind of balance is much harder than it seems. During the base-building phase, we focus heavily on "iron" which plays the role of transporting important compounds like nutrients and oxygen throughout your body, and "healthy fats" that help to smooth out this delivery process.

Iron: While iron has the important role in carrying food nutrients throughout the body, it also carries a much more important cargo: all of the oxygen your body needs to function. A deficiency of iron decreases your red blood cell (hemoglobin) count, meaning parts of your body stop getting as much oxygen as they should. It goes without saying, but this has a negative impact on your body's performance.
Illnesses linked to iron-deficiency)
Brain Anoxia: Dizziness, Lightheadedness, Fainting
Heart Anoxia: Shortness of breath, heart palpitations, chest pain
Muscle Anoxia: Dullness, Fatigue, Stiffness
Appendage Anoxia: Constantly cold fingers and toes

The truth is, many athletes live in a state of "Hidden Anemia." Athletes tend to be much more muscular than normal people, meaning their oxygen requirements, and by extension their iron requirements, are much higher than a typical person's. Athletes also sweat frequently which causes loss of iron, and repeated impacts to the soles of the feet from running and other activities can damage blood vessels and destroy red blood cells, leading to a deficiency of oxygen carriers in the body. We often hear that children require more iron when they are growing, and that some women are highly susceptible to anemia during menstruation, but the risk to men, especially athletes, is also very real.

Healthy Fats: Even if you are being careful with your diet, if your blood flow is slow or your blood vessels are too hard, you won't be able to get the nutrients your body needs to the places it needs them. That's why we also focus on healthy fats that help to promote strong, flexible blood vessels and enable smooth blood flow throughout the body. In particular, the good fats we talk about here are Omega 3 fatty acids like EPA and DHA, which are found abundantly in fish.

Although our image of fat is usually negative, healthy fat is crucial for athletes to maintain consistently high performance. So rather than cutting fat, let's work to improve the quality of the fat in our diet instead. As a first step, it's best to avoid fried foods and fatty meats, and instead utilize ingredients with lots of Omega 3 fatty acids. With just this small change, you can take a huge step forward in your diet without reducing the amount you eat at all.

POWER UP

パワーアップ

体は、筋肉をはじめ頭の先から足の爪まで、多くはたんぱく質でできています。そしてすべての細胞は分解と再生をくり返して、日々生まれ変わっていきますので、日頃から質の良いたんぱく質をとる習慣が、細胞レベルから質の高い体を作っていくことになります。

特に、運動によっていたんだ筋肉を回復させることに意識を向けてみましょう。食事の中にたんぱく質が十分にあると、筋肉の生まれ変わりを助け、強くてしなやかな筋肉を作ることにつながる一方で、たんぱく質が足りていないと、筋肉を分解し減少していくといわれています。

運動習慣のない人でも、筋肉やそれ以外の細胞が一定の速度で生まれ変わるのは同じです。良質なたんぱく質をとることが、肌ツヤ髪ツヤなどにつながり、体のすみずみまで健康的でイキイキ輝く秘訣となります。私の例をあげると、明らかに肌の調子が安定しました。保水量も増え、肌荒れもほとんどなくなったのが、心の安定をもたらしてくれています。このように、作り手にもうれしい変化がみられるのも続けたくなる理由です。

しかし、ただやみくもに量をとれば良いわけではありません。ここで言うたんぱく質というのは、ムダとムラがない状態の「質の良いたんぱく質」のこと。つまり、村田家のルールひとつめの「たんぱく源は2種類以上入れること」で、その質を高めているのです。

2種類以上のたんぱく源は、特性が異なるタイプから取り入れることをおすすめしています。厳密には、アミノ酸スコアを高めるためには、おたがいのスコアを補うような食べ合わせが好ましいと思いますが、無数にある食材の各値を把握することはできませんので、目で見て選べるように、私なりにたんぱく源を4つに分類しています。

赤のたんぱく源
酸素を全身に運ぶ赤血球（ヘモグロビン）を作る「鉄分」が豊富
㊎牛肉、赤魚（まぐろ、かつお）

白のたんぱく源
脂質が少なく、体を構成する「たんぱく質」が豊富
㊎鶏肉、白魚（鯛、たら）、豆、豆腐

ピンクのたんぱく源
主なエネルギー源となる糖質の分解を助ける「ビタミンB_1」が豊富
㊎豚肉、鮭

青のたんぱく源
血液をサラサラにする「良質な脂質」が豊富
㊎青魚（いわし、あじ、さんま）

一番に大切にしている思いが「トレーニングの成果を、食事でムダにしたくない」ということ。運動後の食事次第で、過酷なトレーニングの成果は大きく左右されます。運動後の食事の質を上げるためのひとつめは「パワーアップ」、運動によっていたんだ筋肉を回復させることです。

Because your training results can fluctuate dramatically based on your post-exercise nutrition, I'm always careful to avoid wasting the results of hard training with the food I make. Recipes designed for powering up focus on bringing out the maximum muscle recovery to help get the most out of a top-tier training regimen.

From the top of your head to the tips of your toes, your body, including all of your muscles, is mostly made of proteins. And because your cells are constantly going through the rebirth cycle of dividing and reassembling, providing your body with a steady supply of the best protein building materials will help you build a strong body starting from the cellular level.

In particular, let's focus on the process of rebuilding the muscle fibers that have been broken down by intense exercise. If you're getting enough protein from the food you eat, it will aid in the regeneration of your muscles, promoting strong and flexible muscle fibers. On the other hand, if you're not eating enough quality protein, there's some evidence that it can actually prevent your muscles from recovering properly, and DECREASE your muscle tissue instead.

Even for people without a consistent exercise regimen, your cell's life cycles remain the same. Consuming good protein helps to promote healthy hair and skin, and is the secret to achieving a healthy, glowing complexion. For me personally, monitoring my protein intake has helped to strengthen my skin immensely. Skin dryness and roughness which are issues that erode the self-confidence of many women, have mostly gone away. Unsurprisingly, seeing my own great results makes it a lot easier to commit to maintaining my whole family's nutrition.

However, protein intake is not only about blindly consuming as much protein as you can. The protein I've been referring to thus far is a well-balanced portion of "High Quality Proteins." In other words, Rule 1 of my three rules (Include at least two types of protein) is the secret to maintaining high protein ***quality*** in your diet.

When you choose your two types of protein, I suggest that you make two selections that are relatively different from one another. Strictly speaking, the best way to achieve the highest Amino Score would be to carefully compare the Amino Scores of all your component proteins, but with the countless options for protein-filled ingredients this can border on impossible. That's why, rather than amino acids, I've divided protein sources into the following four categories, which you can identify just by looking at them.

RED PROTEINS
Rich in iron, which aids in the creation of red blood cells
ⓔⓧ Beef, Red Fish (Tuna, Katsuo)

WHITE PROTEINS
Low in fat, and high in body building protein
ⓔⓧ Chicken, White fish (Seabream, Cod), Beans, Tofu

PINK PROTEINS
High in Vitamin B_1, which aids in the breakdown of carbohydrates for energy
ⓔⓧ Pork, Salmon

BLUE PROTEINS
High in healthy fats, which aid in blood flow and strengthens blood vessels
ⓔⓧ Blue Fish (Sardines, Mackerel, Saury)

POWER CHARGE
パワーチャージ

エネルギーは原動力。足りていないと、思い通りに体が動きませんし、疲労感も抜けません。活動前にはこれから使うぶんを、活動後には失ったぶんを、しっかりと補うことで、パフォーマンスアップや疲労感の抜けの早さ、超回復や筋力アップにもつながります。

炭水化物・たんぱく質・脂質はいずれもエネルギー源になる役割を持っていますが、私たちは、まず炭水化物に多くふくまれる糖質をエネルギー源として使います。糖質は、体内で生命維持や運動のために使われ、脳や内臓など体じゅうの器官や組織にエネルギーを供給します。この糖質の量が少ないと、次にエネルギーになりやすいたんぱく質からエネルギーを生み出すことになり、たんぱく質本来の目的だった細胞の生まれ変わりに十分に充てることができないのです。

さらに、運動をするとエネルギー消費は増えるので、運動前に十分に糖質量を摂取できていないと、運動中にエネルギー切れを起こしてバテたり、感情コントロールがきかずイライラしたり、集中力が低下して怪我をするリスクも増えます。そして、運動後のすばやい糖質補給は、体の回復を助けることにつながります。

スポーツ栄養学を通じて出会ったのが「食事でパフォーマンスは変わる」という考え方です。パフォーマンスの大切さは、アスリートではない一般人も同じ。今日１日、元気に、ごきげんに過ごせるかどうかなど、日常生活のパフォーマンスを高めたいもの。

一方でスポーツを生業とするアスリートの場合、パフォーマンスのばらつきが命取りになる可能性もあります。資本である体を健康に保ち（ベースメイク）、強くし（パワーアップ）、さらにプレーで活躍するための原動力をためておく（パワーチャージ）の３ステップで、ベストな状態を保つ努力をしています。

今までご紹介したことは、残念ながら、明日すぐに結果が出るものではなく、継続の先に、ふと「そういえば最近調子が良いな」と気づくものだと考えています。大切なのは、食事ではなく食習慣。ジャンクフードを食べることが悪いわけではなく、食べ続けることが良くないのです。

日々の体の変化に耳を傾けながら、みなさんのライフスタイルの中で無理のない範囲でこつこつと続けてみましょう。

そしてもうひとつは「パワーチャージ」、運動によって失ったエネルギーを回復させること。「運動後の食事の質を上げること」ができたら、「運動でのパフォーマンスを上げる食事」、「運動をし続けられる体づくりのための食事」へとGOOD HABITの道は続いていくのです。

Lastly, we'll look at revitalizing yourself and raising your energy levels through exercise. By increasing the quality of your post-exercise nutrition, we can create meals that increase performance and create a body capable of sustaining high levels of output for a long period of time, all through the simple application of our GOOD HABIT framework.

As you already know, energy is the driving force for anything we do. If you don't have enough, your body won't move the way you want it to, and you'll be left with a lingering fatigue and tiredness. By compensating for your energy expenditure with your pre and post-workout nutrition, you can recover from fatigue faster and improve your muscle strength and recovery.

Our body can create energy by breaking down carbohydrates, proteins, or fats, but our go-to source of energy is the abundant sugars found in carbohydrate-rich foods. Carbohydrates are the energy source for your body's normal functions as well as all of your exercise, and are the preferred energy unit for not only muscle, but also your brain and internal organs. If you don't have enough carbs in your diet, then your body will use its next energy preference; proteins. However, as you've probably guessed, the proteins your body breaks down for energy then become unavailable for their original use as the crucial building blocks for your cell and muscle regeneration.

Furthermore, since exercise expends high amounts of energy, insufficient carbohydrate intake can lead to burnout during training, increased irritability and emotional instability, and a decrease in concentration and precision over time. For post-workout as well, a lack of carbohydrates can impede your recovery and lead to further energy deficits for your next workout.

In my study of sports nutrition, I encountered the idea of "altering performance through diet." And whether we acknowledge it or not, performing at your top level is just as important for everyday people as it is for professional athletes. High performance in our daily lives is often linked to such crucial concerns as our overall health and energy, and how long and often we can maintain a good mood.

In the case of athletes that make their living through sports, inconsistency in performance can be career-ending. This is why our household pays close attention to the three steps of creating a strong base, stimulating growth in muscle mass and strength, and increasing the body's energy capacity and ability to function at a high level for a sustained period. Paying attention to all of these is how we keep my husband in the best shape possible to perform.

Of course, none of the concepts or strategies that I have shared here will yield results overnight. Instead, by following them consistently, you will eventually wake up one day and realize that your body feels better than it ever has before. What's important is not the individual meals and their components, but the dietary habits that you create and incorporate into your lifestyle. In the same way, eating one piece of junk food is not the end of the world. Eating it every day though can lead you down a dark road.

The best way to proceed forward is by paying attention to the way that your body changes and responds to your GOOD HABITs. That's the best way to make changes that will last.

CHAPTER 1

MAK

体の土台を整えたいときは、“鉄分と良質な脂質を多くふくむ食材を使う”こと。
鉄を効率よく体内へ吸収するために、肉類や魚介類などの動物性食品に多い吸収率の高いヘム鉄と、植物性食品や緑黄色野菜、卵などに多い吸収率の低い非ヘム鉄のどちらもバランスよく組み合わせて。
おすすめしたい良質な脂質、オメガ３系の脂肪酸を多くふくむのは、いわしやさばなどの青魚や、アマニ油やえごま油。酸化しないように、加熱をおさえてフレッシュな状態で食卓に取り入れましょう。今よりもっと快適で動ける体へ。

ING A BASE

ベースメイク

When building a solid nutritional foundation, you should start with foods high in iron and healthy fats.
In order to efficiently absorb iron throughout the body it's important to have a balanced intake of both the high absorption, heme iron found in animal foods such as meat and fish, and the low absorption, non-heme iron found in green and yellow vegetables or eggs.
For healthy fats, I recommend blueback fish (sardine or mackerel), flaxseed oil, or sesame oil, all of which are high in omega 3 fatty acids. To avoid oxidation, avoid over-heating and try to serve these in as fresh a state as possible.
These building blocks will help you create a more comfortable and mobile body.

LAMB CHOPS

When my husband lived in New Zealand, we got to experience all sorts of new lamb recipes. We don't use lamb at all in traditional Japanese cooking, but as a healthy meat option we were happy to bring this recipe home with us. By using residual heat in the pan, you can soften the meat and keep it juicy, and it goes great with a refreshing basil sauce.

家で気軽に味わえる本場の味。
余熱でジューシーに仕上げたラム
大きな口でかぶりついてめしあがれ。

ラムチョップ

材料

2人分

ラムチョップ …… 4本(400g)
塩／粗挽き黒こしょう …… 各少々
ズッキーニ(緑・黄) …… 各1/2本
サラダ油 …… 各少々

バジルマスタードソース

バジル(みじん切り) …… 8枚
粒マスタード …… 大さじ1
はちみつ …… 小さじ1

作り方

1. ラムチョップは塩、粗挽き黒こしょうをふる。ズッキーニは1cm幅の輪切りにする。ソースの材料を合わせておく。

2. グリルパンにサラダ油を薄く塗って中火で熱し、ズッキーニの両面をこんがりと焼き色がつくまで焼いて取り出す。

3. 続いてラムチョップを、トングで押さえて脂身を下にして立てるようにして並べ、脂身に焼き色がついたら肉を寝かせ、片面3分ずつ焼く。ふたをして火を止め、5～6分おいて余熱で火を通す。(2)とともに器に盛り、ソースをかける。

INGREDIENTS

FOR TWO

Lamb chop …… 4 (400g)
Salt and freshly ground black pepper
Zucchini, green and yellow …… 1/2 each
Vegetable oil

Basil mustard sauce

Basil, finely chopped …… 8 leaves
Grain mustard …… 1 tablespoon
Honey …… 1 teaspoon

HOW TO MAKE

1. Season lamb chops well with salt and ground pepper. Cut zucchini into round slices. Mix the ingredients for the basil mustard sauce.

2. Heat oil in a pan over medium heat. Cook zucchini until both sides are golden brown.

3. Add the lamb chops to the pan, starting with fat side down (hold in place using tongs if necessary). When the fat side is browned, grill the other sides of the meat, roughly 3 minutes on each side. Turn off the heat and use the residual heat to cook the meat through, which will take roughly 5-6 minutes. To serve, plate with zucchini and add basil mustard sauce to taste.

TIPS

羊肉は「ベースメイク」の基本となる鉄分や良質な脂質を多くふくむうえに、脂肪の燃焼をうながすアミノ酸由来のLカルニチンも豊富で、太りにくい体づくりを助けます。香りが気になる場合は、しょうゆ・酒・しょうがで下味をつけて。

Lamb is a great source of protein and healthy oils (unsaturated fatty acids) and helps promote blood flow. Lamb also includes rich carnitine that burns fat, and includes iron that not only increases recovery from fatigue, but also prevents or improves anemia.

いわし缶だけで、味つけいらず。
うまみと栄養がぎゅっと濃縮した
水煮缶の汁はつけ合わせのお味噌汁に。

いわしバーグ

SARDINE BURGE

If you want to eat more fish, but find raw fish cuts intimidating, canned fish can be a great option since it has less hassle while maintaining nutritional value. The sardine's have enough saltiness that you won't need to add a lot of excess seasoning, but you can add a splash of lemon or lime juice for extra flavor if you'd like.

材料

2人分（4個分）

いわし水煮缶	2缶（150g×2）
絹ごし豆腐	60 g
青じそ	4枚
片栗粉	大さじ1
サラダ油	少々

作り方

1. いわし缶は汁けをきる。
2. ボウルにいわし、豆腐、片栗粉を入れ、スプーンの背でいわしをつぶしながらよく混ぜる。4等分して平たい丸形にまとめ、青じそを1枚ずつ貼りつける。
3. フライパンに油を熱し、(2)を青じその面を下にして並べる。両面にこんがり焼き色がつくまで2分くらいずつ焼く。

INGREDIENTS

FOR TWO (FOUR PIECES)

Canned boiled sardine	2 (150g x 2)
Silk tofu	60g
Green shiso leaves	4
Katakuri powder (potato starch)	1 tablespoon
Vegetable oil	

HOW TO MAKE

1. Drain the excess liquid from the canned boiled sardine. (This liquid can be saved and used with miso soup as a flavor enhancer if you would like.)
2. Add the sardines, tofu, and potato starch to a bowl, and mix well by crushing the sardine using the back of a spoon. Divide the mixed ingredients into 4 portions, shape into patties, and top with green shiso leaves.
3. Heat oil in the pan, and grill (2) starting with the green shiso leaves face-down in the pan. Cook until both sides are golden brown, about 2 minutes.

TIPS

いわし水煮缶は良い食習慣のスタートに、まず取り入れてほしい優秀食材。下ごしらえが必要ないだけでなく、実は生の状態よりも鉄分やカルシウムなどの不足しがちな栄養素をアップしています。やわらかめの生地も、青じそでまとめやすく。

Sardines contain high quality protein, oil, and iron, and using canned sardines avoids the messy process of cutting open the fish. Canned sardines also have softer bones which you can eat easily, adding more calcium to the dish. I highly recommend keeping some canned sardines in your pantry!

MACKEREL PAELLA

Super colorful, and full of flavor, this dish is a great and filling way to add color to the table for dinner parties. For a more flavorful dish, use more of the excess liquid from the mackerel can, but make sure to mix it in well before eating.

見た目にも華やかで、できたてを
そのまま食卓へ届けたい一品。
目の前で仕上げる瞬間がお楽しみ。

さば缶パエリア

材料

作りやすい分量

さば水煮缶	1缶(190g)
ミニトマト	8個
玉ねぎ	1/2個
豆苗	1/2束
米	2合
顆粒コンソメ	小さじ1
にんにく(みじん切り)	2片分
オリーブ油	大さじ1
ローリエ	1枚
レモン	適量

作り方

1. さば缶は身と缶汁を分ける。缶汁は水を加えて390mlにし、コンソメを加えて溶かす。

2. 玉ねぎは1cm角に切る。豆苗は1〜2cm幅に切る。

3. 直径26cmほどのフライパンにオリーブ油とにんにくを入れて中火で熱し、香りが立ったら玉ねぎを加え、透き通るまで炒める。

4. 米を洗わずに加えて炒め、油がまわったら(1)を加える。ミニトマト、さばの身をのせ、ローリエを加えてふたをして弱火で20分ほど煮る。火を止めてそのまま5分ほどおき、豆苗をのせる。くし形に切ったレモンを添える。

INGREDIENTS

EASY TO MAKE AMOUNT

Canned boiled mackerel	1 (190g)
Cherry tomatoes	8
Onion	1/2
Tomyo (bean seedling)	1/2 package
White rice	2 cups (300g)
Powder consommé (beef bouillon)	1 teaspoon
Garlic, finely chopped	2 cloves
Olive oil	1 tablespoon
Bay leaf	1
Lemon	

HOW TO MAKE

1. Drain the canned mackerel fish, and save your preferred quantity of the canning liquid. Add water to this liquid up to 390ml, and add consommé to make a soup that can be served on the side.

2. Dice onions into 1cm cubes, and chop the bean seedlings to roughly 1-2cm.

3. Heat a large (roughly 26cm) pan over medium heat, and lightly fry garlic with olive oil. Add onion when the garlic begins to fragrant, and cook until the onions become translucent.

4. Toast uncooked rice without washing, and add the soup from (1) when the rice is well mixed with the oil. Add cherry tomatoes, canned mackerel and bay leaf, cover and let simmer on low heat for 20 minutes. Turn off the heat and leave it for 5 minutes. Sprinkle bean seedlings over top, and serve with lemon cut into wedges.

TIPS

さば水煮缶の芳醇なうまみをたっぷり吸ったごはんは栄養の宝庫。強い抗酸化作用を持つミニトマトや豆苗が、さばの良質な脂質をはじめとした高い栄養価をさらに後押しします。豆苗は最後に加えて、食感を残し、彩りよく仕上げましょう。

Canned mackerel contains healthy oils such as DHA and EPA, and helps improve the flexibility of blood vessels. Cherry tomatoes have good antioxidant effects, and bean seedlings have vitamins that help your body to absorb the oils from the mackerel. Waiting to add the bean seedlings until directly before eating adds a nice texture and color to the dish.

JAPANESE RICE GRATIN

This s a no-fuss gratin dish that involves simply stirring in a light, tofu-based sauce. A quick, simple, and healthy dish that's best served hot.

豆腐で作る軽やかなホワイトソースと
磯の香りが食欲をそそります。
アツアツのうちにめしあがれ。

和風ドリア

材料

2人分

温かいごはん	400g
桜えび	大さじ2
青のり	大さじ1
ピザ用チーズ	60g
粉チーズ	大さじ2

豆腐ソース

絹ごし豆腐	1/2丁（150g）
みそ	小さじ1

作り方

1. オーブンを200℃に予熱しておく。
ボウルにごはんを入れ、桜えび、青のりを加えて混ぜ、耐熱の器に盛る。

2. 別のボウルに豆腐ソースの材料を入れ、スプーンでつぶしながらなめらかに混ぜる。(1)にかける。

3. ピザ用チーズ、粉チーズをふり、オーブンで10分ほど、焼き色がつくまで焼く。

INGREDIENTS

FOR TWO

Steamed rice	400g
Sakura Ebi (dried small shrimps)	2 tablespoon
Aonori (dried seaweed flakes)	1 tablespoon
Cheese mix for pizza	60g
Grated parmesan cheese	2 tablespoon

Tofu sauce

Silk tofu	1/2 package (150g)
Miso	1 teaspoon

HOW TO MAKE

1. Pre-heat the oven to 200°C.
Mix rice, dried small shrimps, and dried seaweed flakes in a bowl, and place in the baking dish.

2. Mix the tofu-sauce in a separate bowl by combining all ingredients and mashing with a spoon to smoothen the mixture. Add the sauce to the baking dish from (1).

3. Sprinkle cheese mix and parmesan cheese, and place the dish in the preheated oven. Bake for about 10 minutes until the cheese is melted and golden.

TIPS

バター、小麦粉、牛乳で作る定番のホワイトソースは高脂質になりがち。豆腐にみそを合わせ、あっさりとしながらもコクのある簡単なソースにアレンジしました。ストック食材の桜えびや青のりで、香ばしさとミネラルをプラス。

The white sauce you typically use in gratin contains ingredients like butter, flour, and milk, creating a high-fat, high-calorie mixture. This white sauce is made from tofu and miso, which is light yet rich in flavor. The dried shrimps and dried seaweed flakes add calcium and savoriness, and I always have them on-hand in my kitchen.

野菜たっぷり、一品でも大満足のごちそうに。
焼きながらいただく楽しさも、栄養のうちです。

HOTPLATE BIBIMBAP

A dish full of vegetables that's sure to leave the whole table feeling happy and satisfied. The fun of grilling on a hotplate is just one more thing to be excited about for this nutritious meal.

ホットプレートビビンバ

材料

2人分

牛ひき肉		200 g
ほうれん草		3株
にんじん		1/2本
もやし		1袋
焼肉のたれ(市販)		大さじ2
A	ごま油	大さじ1
	鶏ガラスープの素(顆粒)	小さじ1/2
	塩/おろしにんにく	各少々
温かいごはん		400 g
卵		1個
白いりごま		大さじ1

コチュジャンだれ

コチュジャン/しょうゆ/白すりごま	各大さじ1
はちみつ	大さじ1/2
水	大さじ1

作り方

1. ほうれん草は4〜5cm長さに切る。にんじんは細切りにする。A、コチュジャンだれの材料を合わせておく。

2. ほうれん草は30秒ほど、もやしは40秒ほど、にんじんは1分ほど蒸し煮にし(37ページ参照)、それぞれAを1/3量ずつからめて30分ほどおく。

3. フライパンを油をひかずに中火で熱し、ひき肉を炒め、色が変わったら焼肉のたれで調味する。

4. ホットプレートを200℃に熱し、ごはんを広げる。(2)、(3)をバランスよくのせ、真ん中に卵を割り入れる。白ごまをふる。全体を混ぜ、好みの加減に焼き、好みでたれを添えて食べる。

INGREDIENTS

FOR TWO

Beef, minced		200g
Spinach		3 bunches
Carrot		1/2
Bean sprouts		1 package
Yakiniku sauce		2 tablespoons
A	Sesame oil	1 tablespoon
	Powder chicken consommé (chicken stock powder)	1/2 teaspoon
	Salt, Grated garlic	
Steamed rice		400g
Egg		1
White sesame		1 tablespoon

Gochujang sauce

Gochujang, Soy sauce, White grated sesame	1 tablespoon
Honey	1/2 tablespoon
Water	1 tablespoon

HOW TO MAKE

1. Chop the spinach to 4-5cm, and slice the carrots thinly. Mix A and gochujang sauce ingredients together in a separate bowl.

2. Steam your vegetables : spinach for 30 seconds, 40 seconds for bean sprouts, and 1 minute for carrots. Stir in 1/3 of the A sauce each and let rest for 30 minutes.

3. Heat an unoiled pan over medium heat, and cook the minced beef, adding yakiniku sauce when the meat begins to brown.

4. Heat the hotplate to 200°C , and spread the rice. Add (2) and (3) to the hotplate, and put the egg in the middle, sprinkling white sesame to preference. Mix all of the rice and other ingredients, and grill as long as you would like. Add the remaining sauce as desired.

TIPS

炭水化物、たんぱく質、ビタミンなどが一度にバランスよくとれる一品です。野菜の脂溶性ビタミンは油脂類と合わせることで吸収率アップ。ホットプレートを囲み、好みの加減に焼き目をつけながら食べるのも楽しく、食が進みます。

Bibimbap is a well-balanced dish full of carbohydrates, protein, and vitamins, and by mixing the vegetables with oil, you increase your body's vitamin absorption. This can technically be cooked in a pan, but the fun of cooking it on a big hotplate provides a fun experience to go with your delicious dinner.

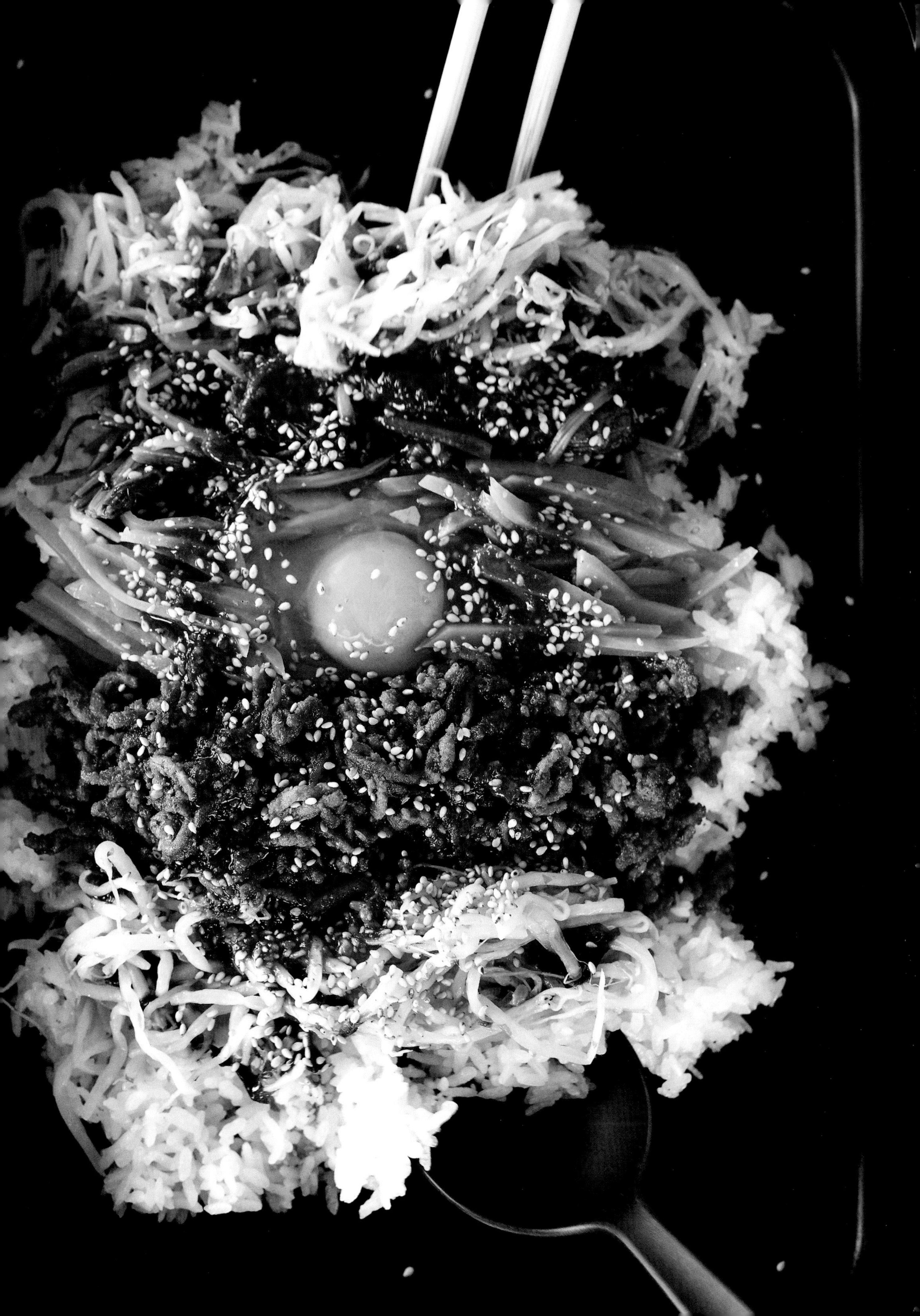

ラガーマンの体を育んだお母さん直伝の味。
色とりどりの野菜のうまみが溶け込んでいます。

HAYASHI RICE, HASHED BEEF

One of my mother-in-law's most beloved dishes. It locks in all the flavor and nutrients of a variety of vegetables into one delicious package, which is rare for hayashi rice.

さえこさんのハヤシライス

材料

4人分

牛こま切れ肉		300g
玉ねぎ		1個
えのきだけ		1/2袋
しいたけ		3個
にんじん		1/2本
ピーマン		3個
にんにく(みじん切り)		1片分
バター		20g
A	デミグラスソース缶	1缶(290g)
	トマトジュース(無糖、無塩)	200ml
	顆粒コンソメ	大さじ1
	ウスターソース	小さじ1
	砂糖(黒糖、三温糖など)	小さじ1
	ローリエ	1枚

INGREDIENTS

FOR FOUR

Beef, chopped		300g
Onion		1
Enoki mushroom		1/2 handful
Shiitake mushrooms		3
Carrot		1/2
Green pepper		3
Garlic, finely chopped		1 clove
Butter		20g
A	Canned Demi-glace sauce	1 (290g)
	Sugar-free, unsalted tomato juice	200ml
	Powder consommé (beef bouillon)	1 tablespoon
	Worcestershire sauce	1 teaspoon
	Sugar	1 teaspoon
	Bay leaf	1

作り方

1. 玉ねぎは薄切りにする。えのきだけは半分に切る。しいたけは石づきを落として薄切りにする。にんじん、ピーマンは細切りにする。

2. 鍋にバターとにんにくを入れて中火で熱し、香りが立ったら玉ねぎを加え、透き通るまで炒める。牛肉を加え、色が半分変わるくらいまで炒める。

3. (1)の残りの野菜を加えてひと炒めし、Aを加え、弱火で20分ほど煮る。温かいごはん(分量外)を器に盛り、かける。

HOW TO MAKE

1. Slice onion thinly, and cut enoki mushrooms in half. Slice shiitake mushrooms after cutting off the stem. Slice carrots and green pepper to your preferred size.

2. Heat butter and garlic in a pan over medium heat. Once the flavor has been brought out, add onions and toss until onions become translucent. Add beef into the pan, and stir until beef is cooked halfway through.

3. Add the other vegetables of (1), and the sauce components from A, and simmer for about 20 minutes on low heat. Serve over warm rice.

TIPS

牛肉と玉ねぎで作る定番のハヤシライスに、たっぷりの野菜を加えて、おいしさと栄養価をアップ。煮込んでかさが減ることでたくさんとれるうえ、野菜が苦手な子どもたちにも食べやすくなります。夫の食べ親しんだ味に、ルウを使わず脂質量をおさえるひと工夫。

Beef and onions are the typical highlights for hashed beef, but adding a lot of vegetables boosts the nutritional value. Simmered vegetables are soft and easy to eat, so kids can eat this even if they typically turn their nose up at vegetables.

SWEET MEETS SALTY
CORO-CORO SALAD

Colorful ingredients are great for your body as well as your appetite, and this salad has plenty of color. The saltiness of the ham and the sweetness of the tomato and kiwi play off each other in this super simple, super tasty salad.

塩けと甘酸っぱさが
絶妙なバランスを生み、
太陽の恵み感じるお手軽で
華やかな一品に。

コロコロサラダ

材料

2人分

生ハム……8枚(50g)
ミニトマト……8個
キウイフルーツ……1個
モッツァレラチーズ(ミニ)……16個(90g)
ミックスナッツ……大さじ1+1/2

ドレッシング

オリーブ油……大さじ1
レモン汁……大さじ1/2
塩/粗びき黒こしょう……各少々

作り方

1. ミニトマトは半分に切る。キウイは7〜8mm厚さのいちょう切りにする。ミックスナッツは粗く刻む。
2. ボウルにドレッシングの材料を入れ、泡立て器でよく混ぜる。(1)、生ハム、チーズを加えてあえる。

INGREDIENTS

FOR TWO

Dry-cured ham……8 slices (50g)
Cherry tomatoes……8
Kiwi fruit……1
Mozzarella cheese, mini……16 cubes (90g)
Mixed nuts……1+1/2 tablespoon

Dressing

Olive oil……1 tablespoon
Lemon juice……1/2 tablespoon
Salt and freshly ground black pepper

HOW TO MAKE

1. Cut cherry tomatoes into half. Slice kiwi to quarter slices, and chop the nuts for crunchiness.
2. Mix all the dressing ingredients in a bowl, and mix well with a whisk. Toss (1), dry-cured ham, and cheese all together.

TIPS

トマトに多くふくまれる抗酸化作用の強いリコピンは、オリーブ油と一緒にとると効果的といわれています。生ハムとチーズという2種類のたんぱく源に、トマトとキウイのたっぷりのビタミン類が合わさり、彩りの良さに加えて、栄養価も高く、さらに満足な食べごたえもあるサラダに。

The antioxidant lycopene is abundant in tomatoes and is found to have a better absorption rate when consumed with olive oil. This salad is a great nutritional option thanks to the combination of two types of protein (cured ham and cheese), and the plentiful vitamins in tomato and kiwi.

CUMIN COLESLAW

To let all of the flavors mix together, it's best to leave sitting for at least 15 minutes after mixing.The cumin-based dressing goes very well with corn or red cabbage as well.

コールスローとはオランダ語で
キャベツのサラダのこと。
スパイスの風味をきかせるのが
お気に入り。

クミン風味のコールスローサラダ

材料

2人分

キャベツ 3枚
にんじん 1/3本

ドレッシング

プレーンヨーグルト（無糖） 大さじ6
オリーブ油 大さじ1
レモン汁 大さじ1
クミンシード 小さじ1
塩／粗挽き黒こしょう 各少々

作り方

1. キャベツ、にんじんはせん切りにする。
2. ボウルにドレッシングの材料を入れ、泡立て器でよく混ぜる。(1)を加えてあえる。ドレッシングとあえてから、15分ほどおくと味がよりなじむ。

INGREDIENTS

FOR TWO

Cabbage 3 leaves
Carrot 1/3

Dressing

Non-sugar plain yogurt 6 tablespoons
Olive oil 1 tablespoon
Lemon juice 1 tablespoon
Cumin seeds 1 teaspoon
Salt and freshly ground black pepper

HOW TO MAKE

1. Slice cabbages and carrots thinly.
2. Mix all the dressing ingredients in a bowl with a whisk. Toss together with (1).

TIPS

クミンは消化を促進する効果が期待できるスパイス。シード（種）のプチプチとした食感もアクセントになります。食物繊維が豊富なキャベツや、乳酸菌が豊富なヨーグルトと合わせるので、腸内をリセットしたいときにおすすめ。

Cumin is a spice that helps to settle any stomach issues and promote regularity, while also adding great flavor and texture accents. The cabbage also has plenty of fiber, which helps a lot when you need a stomach "reset."

CARROT RAPPE

The sweetness of the carrots and raisins pairs well with the fattiness from the nuts and oil. Rather than the sourness common in other rappe recipe, this focuses instead on elevating that sweetness. This dish keeps well in the fridge, so make a lot to use over multiple meals.

レモンを使わずに
まろやかに仕上げたラペ。
レーズンのフルーティーな
甘みと一緒によくなじませて。

キャロットラペ

材料

2人分

にんじん	1本
レーズン	大さじ2
ミックスナッツ	大さじ2
アマニ油	小さじ1
塩	ふたつまみ

作り方

1. にんじんはせん切りにする。ボウルに入れて塩をまぶし、10分ほどおく。ナッツは粗く刻む。

2. (1)のボウルにレーズン、ナッツ、アマニ油を加え、よく混ぜる。あえてから、15分ほどおくと味がよりなじむ。

INGREDIENTS

FOR TWO

Carrot	1
Raisins	2 tablespoons
Mixed nuts	2 tablespoons
Flaxseed oil	1 teaspoon
Salt	2 dashes

HOW TO MAKE

1. Julienne the carrots. Sprinkle salt, and let rest in a bowl for at least 10 minutes. Chop the nuts for crunchiness.

2. Toss the bowl of (1) adding raisins, mixed nuts and flaxseed oil.

TIPS

にんじんに多くふくまれるビタミンA（β-カロテン）は、油と一緒にとることで効率よく吸収が進みます。またアマニ油やナッツには不飽和脂肪酸（オメガ3系）が豊富で、血流を良くする効果も。ただし酸化しやすいので、加熱せずに使うのがおすすめ。

ß-carotene, which is abundant in carrots, can be absorbed well when combined with oils, and flaxseed oil is an unsaturated fatty acid, which helps to improve blood flow. Because heat will cause excess oxidation, I recommend avoiding any heating of this dish.

A distinctly Japanese arrangement, with komatsuna and dried daikon. This simple dish has deep but subtle flavors, and the dried shrimps add an extra flavor note. Mentsuyu helps make this simple dish even simpler.

ポリポリとした歯ざわりの
切り干し大根がクセになります。
栄養とうまみを逃がさずに
仕上げた定番の味。
めんつゆを使って手軽に。

小松菜と切り干し大根のおひたし

材料

2人分

小松菜	2株
切り干し大根(乾)	5g
桜えび	大さじ1
めんつゆ(ストレート)	大さじ1

作り方

1. 切り干し大根を流水で洗ってざるに上げ、10分ほどおいてから水けを軽くしぼる。
2. 小松菜は半分に切る。フライパンに入れて水大さじ2をふり、強火にかけてふたをして30秒〜1分ほど蒸し煮にする。冷水にとり、水けをしぼって3〜4cm長さに切る。
3. ボウルに(1)、(2)、桜えびを入れ、めんつゆを加えてあえる。

INGREDIENTS

FOR TWO

Komatsuna (Japanese mustard spinach)	2 bunches
Dried daikon (kiriboshi daikon)	5g
Sakura ebi (dried small shrimps)	1 tablespoon
Mentsuyu sauce (noodle soup)	1 tablespoon

HOW TO MAKE

1. Rinse the kiriboshi daikon and let them absorb water for 10 minutes, before squeezing out any excess water.
2. Cut komatsuna in half. Put in a pan over high heat, add 2 tablespoons of water, and steam the komatsuna for 30 seconds to 1 minute. Rinse with ice water, drain well and cut to 3-4cm.
3. Toss (1), (2) and dried small shrimps in a bowl, and mix it with the mentsuyu sauce.

TIPS

小松菜はゆでずにフライパン蒸しに、切り干し大根は水にさらさず、さっと洗うだけといったひと工夫は、栄養の損失をできる限りおさえる調理法で、どんなお料理にも使えます。小松菜、切り干し大根、桜えびは、いずれもカルシウムや鉄分が豊富です。

Komatsuna, dried daikon and dried small shrimp all have high amounts of calcium and iron. By steaming the komatsuna instead of boiling, and lightly rinsing the kiriboshi daikon instead of boiling it or soaking it, you can avoid losing the nutrients in these vegetables.

フライパンで蒸し野菜

毎日350g（おおよそ両手いっぱい分）の野菜を食べることが推奨されていますが、たくさんとるために、たっぷりのお湯でゆでていませんか？そんなときに便利な、野菜の栄養も時間もムダにせず、さらに洗いものも少なくうれしい、良いことづくめの方法をご紹介します。
作り方は簡単。フライパンに洗った野菜を並べ、大さじ２杯程度の水をふり、強火にかけたらふたをして蒸し煮にするだけ。小松菜やおくらなど火が通りやすいものであれば30秒程度、にんじんやかぼちゃなど少し硬いものなら１分程度で、あっというまにおいしい蒸し野菜のできあがり。水分はほとんど使わず、加熱時間も短いので、水溶性ビタミンの流出や加熱に弱いビタミンの損失を最小限におさえられるというすぐれもの。シンプルな調理法だからこそ、野菜本来の味が際立ち、色の鮮やかさも保たれるため、付け合わせにトッピングに食卓をカラフルに彩ります。
家事の合間にさっと仕込めてとにかく万能なので、わが家では多めに作ってストックしています。これだけで毎日の食事の準備がかなり楽になりました。

PAN-STEAMED VEGETABLES

The recommended daily intake of vegetables in 350 grams (roughly two big handfuls), but are you, like many people, boiling your vegetables to make them easier to eat? If that sounds like you, then let me introduce another quick and simple method that also preserves all of the nutrition of your vegetables, and cuts down on the dishes you need to wash afterward.
The method is simple. All you have to do is line up your washed vegetables in a pan, add roughly two tablespoons of water, put over high heat and cover for perfectly steamed vegetables. For quickly cooking veggies like Komatsuna (Japanese mustard spinach) or Okra, 30 seconds is plenty, while sturdier options like carrots or pumpkin should be left on for about a minute. Either way, you'll have delicious steamed veggies in no time at all. This method avoids using excess water and shortens heating time, so you can prevent the loss of highly water-soluble nutrients, as well as vitamins that are weak to high temperatures. Even better, this simple method preserves the flavor and vivid color of your vegetables, making them an excellent way to brighten up your dinner spread as a topping or side dish.
These vegetables are simple and easy to combine with other meals, so I usually make a large stock of them to use later, which makes our daily meal-prep much easier to coordinate.

POWER UP

パワーアップ

細胞の生まれ変わりをうながしたいときは、ムダとムラがない"質の良いたんぱく質をとれる食材を使う"こと。知っておきたい食材選びのヒントは、肉類・魚介類・豆類にふくまれる脂質量。その量が多いほどたんぱく質量は少なく、少ないほどたんぱく質量が多い傾向にあります。たんぱく質の代謝を助けるビタミンB_6をはじめ、ビタミン類も豊富な緑黄色野菜を一緒にとりましょう。彩りを添えることで、目にも体にもおいしい栄養に。すべての選択はもっと強くしなやかな体のために。

To facilitate the smooth and efficient rebuilding of dead cells, we need to focus on using ingredients packed with high-quality protein.
One hint for determining the best ingredients is to take note of the fat content of your chosen meats, fish, or beans. The more fat, the less protein, and vice versa.
Starting with Vitamin B_6, which helps metabolize proteins, we'll also focus on getting lots of vitamins from green and yellow vegetables. These help to add some color to your plate as well as nutrition to your body.
These components work together to help you build a stronger and more supple body.

"TSUKUNE" ASPARAGUS WRAPS
WITH PLUM SAUCE

Plum sauce provides the perfect pairing for this chicken and asparagus dish, and can be used for other dishes as well. Wrapping with shiso leaves helps hold everything together and adds another layer of flavor.

ふわっとやわらかいつくねと
アスパラの食感のかけ合わせが楽しいひと皿。
梅の酸味がきいたたれがマッチします。

アスパラの梅しそつくね

材料

2人分（4本分）

鶏胸ひき肉		200g
グリーンアスパラガス		4本
青じそ		4枚
A	山いも	40g
	青のり	小さじ1/2
	塩／こしょう	各少々
B	梅干し（塩分5%）	3個
	みりん	大さじ1
サラダ油		少々

作り方

1. アスパラガスは根元を落とす。Aの山いもはすりおろす。Bの梅干しは種を除いて耐熱ボウルに入れ、みりんを加えて電子レンジ（600W）で30秒加熱し、梅干しをつぶすように混ぜる。

2. ボウルにひき肉、Aを入れてよく練り混ぜる。4等分してアスパラに巻いて形を整え、それぞれ青じそ1枚で、生地を包み込むように巻く。

3. フライパンにサラダ油を中火で熱し、(2)を並べ、焼き色がついたら裏返し、ふたをして弱火で10分ほど蒸し焼きにする。器に盛り、(1)のたれをかける。

INGREDIENTS

FOR TWO (FOUR PIECES)

Chicken breast, minced		200g
Green asparagus		4
Green shiso leaves		4
A	Yamaimo (Japanese yam)	40g
	Aonori (dried seaweed flakes)	1/2 teaspoon
	Salt and pepper	
B	Umeboshi (pickled Japanese plum)	3
	Mirin	1 tablespoon
Vegetable oil		

HOW TO MAKE

1. Cut the bottom parts near the roots for asparagus. Grate Japanese yam. Prepare sauce by putting the umeboshi in a microwavable bowl, add mirin, heat for 30 seconds in the microwave (600W), and mix well with the softened umeboshi.

2. In another mixing bowl, with clean hands, mix minced chicken and A until well combined. Separate the mince into 4 portions, and shape around the asparagus into a sausage. Wrap this mixture with shiso leaves.

3. Heat a pan over medium heat, and cook (2) until the mincemeat turns brown. Turn them over in the pan, cover and steam for 10 minutes until cooked through. To serve, spoon (1) sauce over the chicken skewer.

TIPS

ふわふわつくねのポイントは山いも。焼く前の生地は、青じそで包み込むように。アスパラには、血管を丈夫にするルチンや、疲労回復効果のあるアスパラギン酸など、栄養が詰まっています。青のりで栄養と彩りをちょい足し。

Chicken is a low fat and lean protein, and the vitamins and fiber from Japanese yam and "Aonori" seaweed enrich its nutritional value even more. The rutin in asparagus which helps strengthen and increase flexibility in body vessels. The contrast of the fluffy texture of the chicken and crispness of the asparagus brings some fun to every bite!

MARLIN SAUTÉ WITH SWEET CHILI SAUCE

"Kajiki" (Marlin) Tuna with a sweet and sour Southeast Asian sauce. A variety of vegetables paired with a low-fat fish makes for a healthy and tasty combination.

しょうがの香る甘酸っぱいソースは
魚にも野菜によく合い
食卓に東南アジアの風を吹かせます。

かじきのエスニック仕立て

材料

2人分

かじき……2切れ
玉ねぎ……1/2個
にんじん……1/3本
ピーマン……1個
えのきだけ……1/4袋
しいたけ……2枚
塩／こしょう……各適宜
片栗粉……大さじ1
ごま油……大さじ1/2

エスニックソース

スイートチリソース／酢／水……各大さじ1
おろししょうが……小さじ1/4

作り方

1. 玉ねぎは縦5mm幅に切る。にんじんは細切り、ピーマンは横に半分に切り、縦に細切りにする。えのきだけは半分に切る。しいたけは薄切りにする。
2. 耐熱容器にエスニックソースの材料を入れ、電子レンジ（600W）で1分加熱する。
3. かじきの水けをキッチンペーパーで取り、塩、こしょう各少々をふる。両面に片栗粉をまぶす。
4. フライパンにごま油を中火で熱し、(1)をしんなりするまで炒め、塩、こしょうをふり、取り出す。続いてごま油少々（分量外）を足して中火で熱し、(3)を並べ、両面にこんがりと焼き色がつくまで焼く。器に盛り合わせ、(2)をかける。

INGREDIENTS

FOR TWO

Marlin……2 pieces
Onion……1/2
Carrot……1/3
Green pepper……1
Enoki mushroom……1/4 handful
Shiitake mushrooms……2
Salt and pepper
Katakuri powder (potato starch)……1 tablespoon
Sesame oil……1/2 tablespoon

Southeast Asian sauce

Sweet chili sauce, Vinegar, Water……1 tablespoon
Ginger, grated……1/4 teaspoon

HOW TO MAKE

1. Slice onions, carrots, and green peppers to 5mm. Cut the enoki mushrooms in half and slice shiitake mushrooms into desired size.
2. Put the ingredients of the sauce in a microwaveable bowl, and heat for 1 minute in the microwave (600W).
3. Drain excess liquid from marlin and season with salt and pepper. Coat both sides of marlin chunks with potato starch.
4. Heat a pan with sesame oil over medium heat, and stir-fry (1) until cooked. Set cooked vegetables aside. Add some more sesame oil to the pan, place (3), and fry to golden. To serve, spoon sauce over the marlin and vegetables.

TIPS

かじきは魚の中でも特にたんぱく質が多く脂質は少なめ、ビタミン、ミネラルも豊富な食材です。火を通しすぎるとパサつきやすいので、片栗粉をまぶして水分が外に流れ出るのを防ぎながら、しっとりと口当たりよく仕上げましょう。

Marlin is one of the best types of lean protein fish, but it dries out easily when overheated. Coating the pieces of fish with potato starch will help soften the mouth feel. You can use a different type of lean protein fish if you like, but make sure to keep the colorful vegetables that add vitamins and minerals to this dish.

PAN-FRIED TOFU WITH JAPANESE TARTAR SAUCE

Pan-fried tofu patties make for a hearty and healthy meat substitute. The tartar sauce is lightened up by using yogurt instead of mayonnaise, and we add a few Japanese seasonings to pair well with the tofu.

カリッと焼いた甘辛い豆腐に
ヨーグルトでさっぱり仕上げた
タルタルソースをたっぷり乗せて。

豆腐ステーキ 和風タルタルソース

材料

2人分

木綿豆腐 …… 1/2丁
片栗粉 …… 大さじ1
ごま油 …… 小さじ1
めんつゆ(ストレート) …… 大さじ2
万能ねぎ(小口切り)/白いりごま …… 各少々

和風タルタルソース

ゆで卵 …… 1個
プレーンヨーグルト(無糖) …… 大さじ2
和風だしの素 …… ふたつまみ
削り節 …… ふたつまみ

作り方

1. 豆腐は4等分に切ってざるにのせ、15分ほどおいて水きりをする。2cm厚さに切り、両面に片栗粉をまぶす。
2. フライパンにごま油を中火で熱し、(1)を並べ、両面に焼き色がつくまで焼く。めんつゆを加えてからめ、器に盛る。
3. ボウルにタルタルソースの材料をすべて入れ、ゆで卵をつぶしながら混ぜる。(2)にかける。

INGREDIENTS

FOR TWO

Momen tofu (firm tofu) …… 1/2 package (150g)
Katakuri powder (potato starch) …… 1 tablespoon
Sesame oil …… 1 teaspoon
Mentsuyu sauce (noodle soup) …… 2 tablespoons
Green onion, finely chopped
White sesame

Japanese tartar sauce

Egg, boiled …… 1
Sugar-free plain yogurt …… 2 tablespoons
Dashi no moto (Japanese dashi powder) …… 2 dashes
Kezuribushi (dried bonito shavings) …… 2 dashes

HOW TO MAKE

1. Cut tofu into 4 pieces and drain for 15 minutes in a strainer. Slice to 2cm thickness, and coat with potato starch on both sides.
2. Heat a pan with sesame oil over medium heat, add (1), and stir-fry both sides until golden. Season with mentsuyu sauce, and serve on a plate.
3. Place all the ingredients of the tartar sauce in a large bowl, and combine well. Spoon over (2) .

TIPS

"畑のお肉"とも呼ばれる豆腐で大豆由来の良質な植物性たんぱく質を補います。片栗粉をまぶすことで、カリッとした焼き目がつき、味もからみやすく。マヨネーズを使わないタルタルソースは、だしや削り節で和風に仕上げます。

Tofu is well known as a vegetable-based protein rich food, and by switching out mayonnaise for the yogurt-based tartar sauce, this tofu dish serves as a healthy and satisfying main course while saving on calories.

A filling and tasty curry that doesn't use prepackaged curry roux. The spiciness of the curry helps you to eat a good amount of vegetables and covers any fishy seafood smell.

魚介とごまの香りがあとを引く変わりカレー。
野菜のうまみでふくらみのある味わいに。

シーフードスパイスカレー

材料

4人分

シーフードミックス（冷凍）	150g
ゆでだこ	150g
ブロッコリー	1/2個
玉ねぎ	1個
ごま油	大さじ2
クミンシード	小さじ1/2
カットトマト缶	1缶（400g）
カレー粉	大さじ1と1/2
塩麹	大さじ2
白すりごま	大さじ2
塩	各少々

作り方

1. 玉ねぎは薄切りにする。たこはぶつ切りにする。シーフードミックスは、流水でさっと洗う。

2. 鍋に湯を沸かし、ブロッコリーを10分ほどゆでてざるに上げる（ゆで汁はとっておく）。粗熱が取れたら、ゆで汁3/4カップとともにフードプロセッサーに入れ、ピューレ状にする。

3. フライパンに、ごま油大さじ1、クミンシードを入れて中火で熱し、軽く色づいてきたら玉ねぎを加え、きつね色になるまで炒める。カットトマト缶を加え、汁けを飛ばすように炒め、カレー粉を加えてなじませる。

4. シーフードミックス、たこを加えてさっと炒め、(2)、塩麹を加えて15分ほど煮る。

5. 残りのごま油、すりごまを加え、塩で味を調える。温かいごはん（分量外）を器に盛り、かける。

INGREDIENTS

FOR FOUR

Seafood mix, frozen	150g
Octopus, boiled	150g
Broccoli	1/2
Onion	1
Sesame oil	2 tablespoons
Cumin seeds	1/2 teaspoon
Canned dice tomatoes	1 (400g)
Curry spice mix powder	1+1/2 tablespoon
Shio koji (salted koji)	2 tablespoons
White ground sesame	2 tablespoons
Salt	

HOW TO MAKE

1. Slice onions thinly. Shave the octopus. Rinse and drain the frozen seafood with water.

2. Boil water in a pot, cook broccoli for 10 minutes and set it aside (keep the boiled water). Once the broccoli has cooled down, puree with a food processor with 3/4 cup of the leftover water.

3. Heat a pan over medium heat, and add 1 teaspoon of sesame oil and cumin seeds. Once browned, add onions and cook to golden. Add canned dice tomatoes, and stir-fry until the liquid cooks off and the mixture has thickened. Add curry spice mix powder and let rest.

4. Stir-fry seafood mix and octopus, mix (2) and salted koji, and simmer for 15 minutes.

5. Add sesame oil and white ground sesame, and salt to taste. Serve over warm rice.

TIPS

ルウで作るカレーは、脂質が多くカロリーオーバーを招きがち。魚介とスパイスに、野菜のピューレやすりごま、塩麹などでコクとうまみが加わり、味わい、食べごたえ、栄養価いずれも満足のいく、体にやさしいひと皿に。

Retail curry roux contains a lot of fat, and typically overloads calories so this dish cuts unneeded oils by using spices instead of roux. Adding vegetable puree, ground sesame and salted koji (fermented Japanese rice paste), bumps up your nutrition intake, not to mention adding lots of flavor.

VEGGIE-PACKED

SPAGHETTI BOLOGNESE

A sweeter, lighter version of Bolognese. The more vegetables you add, the sweeter and more complex the flavor will be. This is great for making ahead of time and saving in the freezer or fridge.

野菜をしっかり炒めて
甘みを引き出してから煮込む、
あっさりこっくりなミートソースです。

スパゲッティボロネーゼ

材料

4人分

鶏むね肉（皮なし）		200g
玉ねぎ		1個
しめじ／にんじん／ほうれん草など好みの野菜		合わせて100g
にんにく（みじん切り）		大1片
オリーブ油		大さじ1
酒		大さじ2
A	カットトマト缶	1缶（400g）
	ウスターソース	大さじ2
	顆粒コンソメ	小さじ1
	ドライオレガノ	小さじ1/2
	ローリエ	1枚
	砂糖	小さじ1
	塩／こしょう	各少々
スパゲッティ		適量

INGREDIENTS

FOR FOUR

Chicken breast, skinless		200g
Onion		1
Vegetables, such as shimeji mushrooms, carrots, spinach		total 100g
Garlic, finely chopped		1 large clove
Olive oil		1 tablespoon
Sake		2 tablespoons
A	Canned diced tomatoes	1 (400g)
	Worcestershire sauce	2 tablespoons
	Powder consommé (beef bouillon)	1 teaspoon
	Dried oregano	1/2 teaspoon
	Bay leaf	1
	Sugar	1 teaspoon
	Salt and freshly ground black pepper	
Spaghetti		

作り方

1. 鶏肉は1cm角に切る。野菜はすべてみじん切りにする。

2. フライパンに、オリーブ油とにんにくを入れて中火で熱し、香りが立ったら玉ねぎを加えて10分ほど炒める。残りの野菜を加えてさらに5分ほど炒め、取り出す。

3. 続いてフライパンを中火で熱し、鶏肉を入れる。少し赤みが残るくらいまで、焼きつけるように炒める。

4. (2)と酒を加えてひと煮立ちしたら、Aを加える。こげつかないようにときどき混ぜながら、弱火で20分ほど煮る。スパゲッティをお好みのかたさにゆでて器に盛り、かける。

HOW TO MAKE

1. Cut the chicken to 1cm dice. Chop all vegetables finely.

2. Heat 1 tablespoon olive oil in a pan over medium heat. Add onion and stir-fry 10 minutes. Add all the vegetables, cook another 5 minutes. Set cooked vegetables aside.

3. Heat the pan over medium heat, and cook chicken until well browned.

4. Add (2) and sake, and add (A). Stir several times not to be burned, and simmer for 20 minutes over weak heat. Cook spaghetti in boiling salted water until al dente. Spoon Bolognese sauce over spaghetti to serve.

TIPS

たくさん作って冷凍しておけば、忙しい場面で頼りになります。冷蔵庫の残り野菜もムダなく使いきれて一石二鳥。オレガノは肉やトマトとの相性が良いスパイスなので、多めに入れても。ひと晩おくと、さらにコクが増します。

With all the hidden vegetables and chicken instead of pork, this version of Bolognese is extra good for you while also being tasty. The sauce itself, as well as extra diced vegetables can be saved in your fridge. You can add more oregano if you would like, or try letting it sit overnight for even better flavor.

RICH FLAVORED SALAD WITH OCTOPUS AND SHUNGIKU

The rich flavor of myoga (Japanese ginger) and sesame oil help to stimulate your appetite. This salad uses a variety of typical Japanese herbs along with octopus for a distinctly Japanese flavor.

生の春菊は苦みがマイルドで、
みょうがやごま油の香りともよく合います。
いつもとひと味ちがうサラダをめしあがれ。

たこと春菊のサラダ

材料

2人分

ゆでだこ……200g
春菊……1/2束(100g)
ミニトマト……3個
A ごま油……大さじ1
A しょうゆ……大さじ1/2
A 塩……ひとつまみ
みょうが……1本
白いりごま……少々

作り方

1. たこは薄切りにする。春菊は1〜2cm幅に切る。ミニトマトは横半分に切って四つ割りにする。
2. みょうがは薄い小口切りにする。Aは合わせておく。
3. ボウルに(1)を入れ、Aを加えてあえる。器に盛り、みょうがをのせ、ごまを散らす。

INGREDIENTS

FOR TWO

Octopus, boiled……200g
Shungiku (Garland chrysanthemum)……1/2 share (100g)
Cherry tomatoes……3
A Sesame oil……1 tablespoon
A Soy sauce……1/2 tablespoon
A Salt……1 dash
Myoga (Japanese ginger)……1
White sesame

HOW TO MAKE

1. Slice octopus as you like. Cut shungiku to 1-2cm. Slice cherry tomatoes into quarters.
2. Slice myoga thinly. Mix all ingredients of (A) well.
3. Put (1) in a bowl and marinate with (A). Serve on a plate and sprinkle myoga and sesame on the top.

TIPS

たこは魚介類の中でも低脂質・高たんぱくの代表格。アミノ酸の一種のタウリンも豊富で、疲労回復や肝臓の解毒作用強化などの効果も。春菊を生でとることで、加熱によるビタミンの損失も防げます。深い緑と赤の色のコントラストが目にもおいしい一品です。

Octopus is one of the top low fat and lean protein seafoods, and shungiku and tomatoes are rich in Vitamin C, which accelerates absorbing that protein effectively. Shungiku is typically used in hotpots, but raw shungiku is actually milder than the bitter taste most people associate it with when it's cooked. This unique salad is a great for kids as well.

たんぱく源は2つ以上入れる

「トレーニングの成果を、食事でムダにしたくない」という思いはこの本の冒頭でもお伝えしました。
運動後に適した質の高い食事。１回の食事で、赤・白・ピンク・青の４色に分類したたんぱく源の中から２色以上を取り入れる献立づくりを紹介します。
わざわざメイン料理を２つも作る必要はありませんのでご安心を。まずメインとなるたんぱく源を決め、サブとしてもう１色を野菜のおかずや汁ものなどに入れていくイメージです。
たとえば、お買い得だった豚肉（ピンク）がメインの日は、いわし（青）のつみれ汁を添えて。旬を迎えたかつお（赤）がメインの日は、蒸し鶏（白）をサラダにトッピングしたり。
お刺身も、４色の分類（赤はまぐろやかつお、白は鯛や平目、ピンクは鮭、青はあじやいわし）にかたよりのない盛り合わせを選べると、より良い栄養バランスに仕上がりますよ。
こうして分類してみると、なんとなく食材の色とイメージが合っています。細かい栄養素まで覚えなくても、目で見て選べる力をつけることが、続けられるGOOD HABITになるのです。

INCLUDING TWO TYPES OF PROTEIN

At the beginning of this book, I mentioned that I am always trying to avoid wasting hard training with improper nutrition. In order to build the best post-workout nutrition, it's best to have at least two of the four protein colors I laid out earlier (red, white, pink, and blue).
Before you worry: no, you don't need to make two main dishes with every meal. Just choose one protein to be your main dish, and add another as an accompaniment to vegetables or soup on the side.
For example, on the day you use pork (pink protein) as your main dish, you can also serve a soup with sardine (blue protein) fishballs. On a day you use tuna (red protein) as your main dish, you can add a little steamed and shredded chicken(white protein) to a salad on the side.
With a plate of sashimi, you can combine all four colors (tuna or katsuo for red, sea bream or flounder for white, salmon for pink, and sardine or mackerel for blue) to get maximum nutritional value.
With this kind of color classification, it becomes much easier to know at a glance what kind of protein each ingredient has. No need for in-depth nutritional knowledge. You can build GOOD HABITs with just your two eyes.

がんばった心身を良い状態に回復するには、効率よくエネルギーを届ける組み合わせで食べること。エネルギー源になる山盛りのごはんには、糖質からのエネルギー生成を進めるビタミンB1を多くふくむ豚肉や鮭をおかずに添えることをお忘れなく。ただし、豚肉は選ぶ部位に気をつけて。ジューシーでも脂質の多い豚バラより、比較的脂質の少ないももやロースを選ぶことで、必要以上の脂質の摂取をおさえられます。ここぞというときにパフォーマンスに、いつもの食事を味方につけて。

To properly restore a tired body, you'll need to eat a combination of foods that delivers energy efficiently.
When you have a heaping helping of energizing rice, don't forget some pork and salmon, which both have large amounts of Vitamin B1 which will help your body process the sugars in the rice.
However, if you pick pork, be careful what cut you pick. Instead of the fatty and juicy pork belly, it's better to pick a lower-fat option like pork loin or thigh meat to avoid excess fat intake.
When it's time for peak performance, you can add these types of options to bolster your normal nutrition.

パワーチャージ

ER CHARGE

“SHABU-STYLE” BOILED PORK WITH FLAVORED TOMATO SAUCE

The sauce goes great with rice since it combines sweetness and a bit of acidity. “Shabu-style” means lightly boiling, so avoid overcooking to ensure soft juicy pork slices.

ほどよい酸味と香ばしさで
食欲の落ちやすい夏場や
ハードな練習後にも
ごはんがすすみます。

豚しゃぶ 香味トマトだれ

材料

2人分

豚しゃぶしゃぶ用肉 …… 300g
酒 …… 大さじ2

香味トマトだれ

トマト …… 1個(120g)
桜えび …… 大さじ1
長ねぎ(みじん切り) …… 20g
にんにく(みじん切り) …… 1片
しょうが(みじん切り) …… 1かけ
しょうゆ …… 大さじ2
酢 …… 大さじ2
砂糖 …… 大さじ1
ごま油 …… 大さじ1/2
鶏ガラスープの素(顆粒) …… 小さじ1

作り方

1. 鍋にたっぷりの湯を沸かし、酒を加える。火を止めて豚肉を1枚ずつ入れ、色が変わるまで余熱で火を通し、ざるに上げて粗熱をとる。
2. トマトは1cm角に切ってボウルに入れ、ほかのたれの材料をすべて加えて混ぜる。15分ほどおいて味をなじませる。
3. 器に(1)を盛り、(2)をかける。

INGREDIENTS

FOR TWO

Pork, thinly sliced …… 300g
Sake …… 2 tablespoons

Flavored tomato sauce

Tomato …… 1 (120g)
Sakura ebi (dried small shrimps) …… 1 tablespoon
Green onion, finely chopped …… 20g
Garlic, finely chopped …… 1 clove
Ginger, finely chopped …… 1 clove
Soy sauce …… 2 tablespoons
Rice vinegar …… 2 tablespoons
Sugar …… 1 tablespoon
Sesame oil …… 1/2 tablespoon
Powder chicken consommé (chicken stock powder) …… 1 teaspoon

HOW TO MAKE

1. Boil water in a pot, and add sake. Turn off the heat, and add pork slices one by one into the pot. Cook pork with the remaining heat of the water until color changes. Set aside and let the meat cool.
2. Chop tomatoes to 1cm dice, put in a bowl, and mix all other sauce ingredients well. Leave it for 15 minutes in order to let the tastes mingle together.
3. To serve, cover the pork and sauce from (2).

TIPS

火を通しすぎるとパサつきやすい豚しゃぶは、余熱でさっと火を通す程度に。定番のねぎだれに、トマトや桜えびを加えて栄養価も風味もアップ。ねぎに豊富なアリシンは、豚肉のビタミンB_1の吸収を高め、疲労物質の乳酸の分解を助けます。

Pork has lots of Vitamin B_1, which helps to change carbohydrates to energy, and promotes that “recharged” feeling from carbs. The dried small shrimp not only adds flavor and crunch, but also adds calcium. This dish is great for summertime or after a hard workout.

PORK VEGGIE WRAP, WITH GINGER SWEET SAUCE

Vegetables wrapped in pork make for a delicious and colorful combination that's fun to eat. The sesame and ginger sauce goes great with all kinds of vegetables, so pick whichever ones you like.

すりごまとしょうがで
いつもの味に香りとコクをプラス。
野菜はお好みのものでどうぞ。

豚肉の野菜巻き しょうが焼き風

材料

2人分

豚ロース薄切り肉 …… 200g
長いも …… 50g
にんじん …… 1/4本
キャベツ …… 1枚(50g)
サラダ油 …… 少々
A めんつゆ(ストレート) …… 大さじ3
　おろししょうが …… 1かけ分
　白すりごま …… 大さじ1

作り方

1. 野菜はそれぞれ細切りにする。Aは合わせておく。
2. 豚肉を1枚ずつ広げ、(1)の野菜をそれぞれ等分にのせてくるくると巻く。
3. フライパンにサラダ油を中火で熱し、(2)の巻き終わりを下にして並べる。ふたをして弱火にし、5分ほど蒸し焼きにする。ふたをはずし、転がしながら焼く。
4. Aを加えてからめる。

INGREDIENTS

FOR TWO

Pork, sliced …… 200g
Yamaimo (Japanese yam) …… 50g
Carrot …… 1/4
Cabbage …… 1 leaf (50g)
Vegetable oil
A Mentsuyu sauce (noodle soup) …… 3 tablespoons
　Ginger, grated …… 1 clove
　White ground sesame …… 1 tablespoon

HOW TO MAKE

1. Slice all vegetables thinly. Mix (A) ingredients well.
2. Divide the (1) vegetables into portions equal to the number of pork slices. Spread each pork slice one by one, wrap vegetables with pork and roll them tightly.
3. Heat a pan with vegetable oil over medium heat, and place in the pan with the seam of the wrap in contact with the pan. Cover, reduce the heat to low, and steam for about 5 minutes. Take off the lid, and cook all the way through.
4. Season with (A) sauce in the pan.

TIPS

野菜を巻いてボリュームアップした豚肉に、しょうががきいたたれが合わされば、ひと口で栄養価も食べごたえも抜群のおかずに。子どものお手伝いとしてもおすすめです。一緒に巻いたり、中の野菜を当てながら食べるのも楽しそう。

Different cuts of pork have different fat content, so try to avoid pork ribs and choose thigh or loin instead. Wrap salad rolls with the pork, and it will not only increase the volume, but adds vitamins and fiber in just one dish.

"OKONOMIYAKI" JAPANESE PANCAKE

Okonomiyaki is one of the most popular Japanese food among foreigners, with a satisfying mix of cabbage and batter. I suggest you eat it like a local, with plenty of special "okonomiyaki sauce."

"お好み"の名のごとく、アレンジ自在。
私が食べ親しんだ神戸の実家の味です。
ちくわとこんにゃくがアクセント。

具だくさんお好み焼き

材料

2人分（2枚分）

- 山いも……50g
- 卵……1個
- だし汁……150ml
- 米粉……100g
- キャベツ……1/8個(140g)
- にんじん……1/4本
- ちくわ……2本
- こんにゃく……50g
- 豚薄切り肉……50g
- シーフードミックス……100g
- 削り節……適量
- サラダ油……少々
- お好み焼き用ソース／マヨネーズ／青のり／削り節(仕上げ用)……各適量

作り方

1. 山いもはすりおろす。キャベツは3cm長さの細切り、にんじんはせん切りに、ちくわは5mm厚さの輪切りにする。こんにゃくは5mm厚さ、5mm×1cm（つきこんにゃくであれば長さ1cm）に切る。
2. シーフードミックスは、流水でさっと洗う。
3. 大きめのボウルに山いも、卵、だし汁を入れ、泡立て器でよく混ぜ、米粉を加えてさらに混ぜる。(1)の具材を加えてよく混ぜる。
4. ホットプレートを200℃に熱し、サラダ油を薄く塗る。(3)を直径20cm、厚さ2cmほどの円形に広げ、削り節をふる。トッピングに、豚肉やシーフードミックスをお好みで並べる。
5. 焼き色がついたら裏返し、さらに4～5分焼く。器に盛り、ソース、マヨネーズ、削り節、青のりをかける。

INGREDIENTS

FOR TWO (TWO PIECES)

- Yamaimo (Japanese yam)……50g
- Egg……1
- Dashi soup……150ml
- Rice flour……100g
- Cabbage……1/8 (140g)
- Carrot……1/4
- Chikuwa (fish sausage)……2
- Konjac……50g
- Pork, sliced……50g
- Seafood mix, frozen……100g
- Kezuribushi (dried bonito shavings)
- Vegetable oil
- Okonomi sauce, fat-free mayo, aonori (dried seaweed flakes), kezuribushi (dried bonito shavings)

HOW TO MAKE

1. Grate the Japanese yam. Shred the cabbage to 3cm, as well as carrots. Cut chikuwa in 5mm thickness, and konjac in 5mm size with 1cm long.
2. Rinse and drain the frozen seafood.
3. Place the Japanese yam, egg and dashi soup in a large bowl, then whisk together well until smooth and well combined. Add rice flour, and mix further. Once smooth, add the ingredients from (1).
4. Pre-heat a hotplate to 200°C, and lightly grease with vegetable oil. Bake (3) into 20cm size pancakes, with a 2cm thickness, and add kezuribushi on top. Make two pancakes, and place pork on one topping, and (2) on top for the other one.
5. Flip over when golden brown, and cook for another 4 to 5 minutes so it is cooked through. To serve, place the okonomiyaki, pour over okonomi sauce, mayonnaise, followed by a sprinkling of aonori and kezuribushi.

TIPS

海外でも人気の高い日本食のひとつが、お好み焼きです。外国の方と一緒にホットプレートを囲んで、焼きながら食べるのもおすすめのコミュニケーション。この一品で、炭水化物、たんぱく質、野菜が一度にとれるバランス食です。

Okonomiyaki means "grill as you like" so feel free to play with the recipe based on your preferences (particularly the chikuwa and konjac that my family loves, but foreigners may not like). If you want to cut fat, you can use low-fat mayonnaise or a spoonful of plain yogurt instead. This all-in-one pancake will fill you with carbohydrate, protein and vegetables.

This super simple, one-pot meal packs great flavor combination from the salmon and mushrooms. Delicious eaten hot and cold, and a great base for onigiri rice balls.

きのことしょうがの香りが
ふわりと広がる炊き込みごはん。
冷めてもおいしく、おにぎりにも。

鮭ときのこの炊き込みごはん

材料

作りやすい分量

- 鮭 …… 大1切れ(125g)
- きのこ
- (しめじ、しいたけなど) …… 合わせて80g
- しょうが(せん切り) …… 2かけ
- ごま油 …… 少々
- A
  - しょうゆ …… 大さじ1
  - 酒 …… 大さじ1
  - みりん …… 大さじ1
  - 和風だしの素 …… 小さじ1
- 米 …… 2合
- 水 …… 370ml
- 青じそ …… 3枚

作り方

1. 米は洗い、ざるに上げる。きのこは食べやすく切る。青じそは1cm角に切る。
2. 鍋にごま油を中火で熱し、しょうが、きのこをさっと炒める。Aで調味する。
3. 米、水を加えてひと混ぜし、鮭をのせる。ふつふつと煮たってきたら、ふたをして弱火で13分炊く。火を止め、そのまま15分蒸らす。
4. 鮭の身をほぐしながら混ぜ、青じそをふる。

INGREDIENTS

EASY TO MAKE AMOUNT

- Salmon …… 1 large filet (125g)
- Mushrooms, such as
- shimeji and shiitake mushrooms …… total 80g
- Ginger, finely chopped …… 2 cloves
- Sesame oil
- A
  - Soy sauce …… 1 tablespoon
  - Sake …… 1 tablespoon
  - Mirin …… 1 tablespoon
  - Dashi no moto
  - (Japanese powder consommé) …… 1 teaspoon
- White rice …… 2 cups (300g)
- Water …… 370ml
- Green shiso leaves …… 3

HOW TO MAKE

1. Rinse and drain the rice. Cut the mushrooms into edible sizes. Chop shiso leaves to 1cm size.
2. Heat a pot with sesame oil over medium heat, and stir-fry ginger and mushrooms. Season with (A) ingredients.
3. Add rice and water to the pot, boil a bit, and place salmon on top. When simmered, place the lid and cook for 13 minutes over low heat. Turn off the heat, and leave 15 minutes as the residual heat will cook it through perfectly.
4. To serve, break up the salmon and mix it all together, then sprinkle shiso leaves on the top.

TIPS

このレシピは鍋で作るものですが、炊飯器でも大丈夫。内釜に米と2合の目盛りまでの水を加え、炒めて味をつけたきのこと鮭をのせて、炊き上げましょう。鮭もきのこもビタミンDを多くふくむので、免疫力アップにも効果的。

Salmon includes high quality protein and also Vitamin B group, which helps recovery of one's body by helping regeneration. It recovers stamina when it is combined together with rice, and can boost your immune system, as both salmon and mushrooms includes plenty of Vitamin D.

PORK FRIED-RICE WITH PICKLED TAKANA

Rice pre-coated with egg before cooking makes for the perfect texture. Takana pickles add a unique Japanese twist to typical fried rice. Once you start eating this, you can't stop until your plate is clean. Enjoy!

卵をからめてから炒めるひと手間で
パラパラごはんに仕上げます。
高菜漬けの風味がほどよい調味料代わりに。

高菜と豚肉のチャーハン

材料

2人分

高菜漬け	80g
豚こま切れ肉	150g
卵	2個
長ねぎ（みじん切り）	8cm
にんにく（みじん切り）	1片
温かいごはん	400g
A しょうゆ	大さじ1/2
A 酒	大さじ1/2
ごま油	小さじ2

作り方

1. 豚肉はAをもみ込み、10分ほどおく。高菜漬けは細かく刻む。ごはんに溶きほぐした卵1個分をからめる。
2. フライパンにごま油小さじ1を中火で熱し、残りの卵を溶きほぐして入れ、さっと炒めて取り出す。続いて残りのごま油とにんにくを入れて中火で熱し、香りが立ったら豚肉、長ねぎ、高菜漬けを加え、豚肉の色が変わるまで炒める。
3. (1)のごはんを加えて炒め合わせ、(2)の卵を戻し入れてひと炒めする。

INGREDIENTS

FOR TWO

Takana pickles	80g
Pork, chopped	150g
Eggs	2
Green onion, finely chopped	8cm
Garlic, finely chopped	1 clove
Steamed rice	400g
A Soy sauce	1/2 tablespoon
A Sake	1/2 tablespoon
Sesame oil	2 teaspoons

HOW TO MAKE

1. Season pork with (A) ingredients, and leave for 10 minutes to marinate. Chop the takana pickles into small pieces. Mix rice with one beaten egg.
2. Heat a pan with 1 tablespoon of sesame oil over medium heat. Stir-fry the other half beaten egg, and set aside. Heat another 1 tablespoon sesame oil and garlic over medium heat, and sizzle. When the smell comes out nicely, add pork, green onion and takana pickles, and cook well until browned.
3. Add the (1) rice and (2) eggs, and stir-fry all together.

TIPS

高菜のお漬物は味が決まりやすいうえに、乳酸菌による発酵効果も加わり、腸を整える効果も。ごはんをパスタに変えてもおいしいです。実家の母がよく作ってくれた思い出の味を少しアレンジしました。料理にお疲れのときにもぜひ。

Takana pickles add a distinct flavor, and the beneficial lactic bacteria from their fermentation is great for your intestinal health. I made this as a variation of one of my favorite home recipes, and highly recommend it when you're a little bit tired of complex cooking. Try switching the rice for pasta for a different take.

COFFEE BREAK

缶詰や乾物は救世主

「まごわやさしい」をそろえるときに活躍するのが、缶詰や乾物。生の状態よりも栄養価が高くなっているものが多く、常温で長期保存がきくので、いざというときのためにもローリングストックしています。何より管理しづらい生もの「さ」の心強い味方。買いものに行けない日も栄養たっぷりのお魚料理を作ることができる、食卓の救世主です。

わが家の定番ラインナップ

缶詰：いわし水煮、さば水煮、ツナ水煮、あさり水煮、ひよこ豆
乾物：桜海老、切干大根、干し椎茸、高野豆腐、わかめ・ひじき・
　　　とろろ昆布などの海藻類

「まごわやさしい」を唱えて、欠けている品目がないか確認するのは、おおかた料理の全体像が見えてきたら。「ご」がなければ、冷奴にすりごまをパラリ、サラダにはナッツをトッピング。「わ」がなければ、お味噌汁に乾燥わかめやとろろ昆布を。そこにしめじも追加して「し」もコンプリート！パズルを埋めていく感覚で気軽にバランスアップできる、魔法のような合言葉です。
地のものを活かしたものが多く、自分へのお土産に買って帰るのも、楽しみのひとつ。

CANNED AND DRIED FOOD SAVE THE DAY

Canned and dried foods are one of my secrets to including all of the Big 7 in our daily nutrition. Many of these options are more nutrient-dense than their raw versions, and they can be stored at room temperature for a long time, so I always keep a stock of them at home.More than anything, canned fish is always much easier to handle than raw fish. Canned fish is a real life-saver on days when you plan to eat fish protein but are too busy to go and buy a fresh catch.

FOR OUR HOUSE, THESE ARE MY GO-TO LINEUP:

Canned: Boiled sardines, Boiled mackerel, Boiled tuna,
Boiled clams, Chickpeas
Dried: Shrimp, Kiriboshi daikon, Shiitake mushrooms, Koya tofu,
and seaweeds of all kinds (Wakame, Hijiki, Shaved konbu, etc.)

To make sure you are including all of our Big 7, it's best to start by taking a step back and look at your meal as a whole. If you see that you're missing sesame, toss a bit on some side tofu, or seeds on a salad. If you're lacking seaweed, you can easily add some wakame to your miso soup on the side. Add some Shimeji mushrooms to the soup as well, and you have another component down! By plugging in the pieces of your nutritional puzzle for each meal, you can easily achieve more balance without any unnecessary hassle.
A lot of regional specialties are typically sold canned or dried as well, so it's a great souvenir to buy for yourself after a vacation.

CHILL OUT

チルアウト

GOOD HABITを長く続ける秘訣は、メリハリ。たまにはふっと力を抜いて、心にも栄養を。
できるだけ果物や野菜を使うことで、自然な甘みの中にうれしい栄養効果も期待できます。特にバナナは、ビタミンやミネラルが豊富。さらに即効性と持続性にすぐれる糖質をふくむため、食の細い子どもやアスリートの補食におすすめ。米粉でもっちりさせたら、心も体もきっと大満足。
お気に入りの一杯を淹れながら、自分と向き合う時間も大切に。

The real key to maintaining your GOOD HABITs in the long-term is being able to wind down from time to time. Occasionally you'll need a break in order to nourish your mind as well as your body.
Through fruits and vegetables, you can get a natural source of sweetness along with some nutritional benefits. In particular bananas are chock full of vitamins and minerals. They also contain sugars and carbohydrates that are quick acting and long lasting, making them a good option for picky kids or as a snack for athletes. Using rice flour adds density to make every sweet and treat extra satisfying.
So grab a cup of your favorite drink and treat yourself a bit. You deserve it!

GLUTEN-FREE BANANA CAKE

I've been making this gluten-free banana cake for my husband since our university days, and it's still his top request when he's craving something sweet.

米粉でもっちり仕上げました。
バナナの甘みと、
ココナッツオイルの風味が
やさしく広がります。

バナナケーキ

材料

18×9×高さ6cmのパウンド型1個分

- バナナ（完熟のもの）……2本
- 米粉……150g
- 牛乳……大さじ2
- 卵……1個
- 三温糖……大さじ2
- ココナッツオイル……大さじ2
- ベーキングパウダー……小さじ2
- くるみ（粗く刻む）……30g
- 塩……ひとつまみ

トッピング

- バナナ……1本
- くるみ……適量

作り方

1. オーブンを180℃に予熱しておく。
ボウルにすべての材料を入れ、泡立て器やゴムべらでバナナをつぶしながらよく混ぜる。
2. 型にオーブンシートを敷き、(1)を流し入れる。薄い輪切りにしたバナナとくるみをのせる。
3. オーブンで50分ほど焼き、爪楊枝をさしてみて生地がついてこなければ焼き上がり。取り出して型に入れたまま冷ます。

INGREDIENTS

FOR 1 BAKING CAKE (18×9×6cm BAKING PAN)

- Bananas, well ripened……2
- Rice flour……150g
- Milk……2 tablespoons
- Egg……1
- Brown sugar……2 tablespoons
- Coconut oil……2 tablespoons
- Baking powder……2 teaspoons
- Walnuts, chopped……30g
- Salt

Toppings

- Banana
- Walnuts

HOW TO MAKE

1. Pre-heat the oven to 180°C.
Put all ingredients in a bowl, and mix well with rubber spatula.
2. Lay out a baking pan with a baking sheet, and pour the batter from (1) into it. Lay sliced bananas and walnuts on top to preference.
3. Bake in the pre-heated oven for 50 minutes, and allow to cool in the mold afterwards.

TIPS

バナナは黒い斑点（シュガースポット）が出たものを使うと、より芳醇な甘さを楽しめます。ふるわずに使える米粉は生地にもっちり感を演出し、グルテンフリーなので混ぜすぎの心配も少ないため、焼き菓子初心者にもおすすめ。

For those who feel intimidated by the words "gluten-free" this is a great starter recipe to show you how easy baking gluten-free sweets can be. Using rice flour as a base helps to make the cake really dense and moist.

COCOA-BANANA SCONES

These are a super simple way to try baking for the first time! Using bananas is healthier than sugar and balances well with the slight bitterness of the cocoa for the perfect level of sweetness.

角切りバターの準備や
成型の手間いらず。
はじめてでも失敗の少ない
スプーンドロップで。

カカオバナナスコーン

材料

約6個分

バナナ		1本(100g)
キヌア(乾燥)		大さじ1
A	米粉	100g
	アーモンドプードル	20g
	黒糖(粉末)	大さじ2
	片栗粉	10g
	ココアパウダー	10g
	ベーキングパウダー	小さじ1
米油		大さじ2
牛乳		大さじ4

作り方

1. オーブンを200℃に予熱する。
ボウルにAを入れ、泡立て器でくるくる混ぜる。米油を加え、粉チーズのようにさらさらになるまで、手ですり混ぜる。

2. 牛乳を加え、スプーンでよく混ぜる。キヌア、バナナを小さくちぎりながら加え、さらに混ぜる。

3. オーブンシートを敷いた天板に、6等分してスプーンでふんわりと落とす。オーブンで15分焼き、天板ごと取り出して冷ます。

INGREDIENTS

FOR SIX PIECES

Banana		1 (100g)
Quinoa, dried		1 tablespoon
A	Rice flour	100g
	Almond flour	20g
	Brown sugar	2 tablespoons
	Katakuri powder (potato starch)	10g
	Cocoa powder	10g
	Baking powder	1 teaspoon
Rice oil		2 tablespoons
Milk		4 tablespoons

HOW TO MAKE

1. Pre-heat the oven to 200°C.
In a large bowl, mix (A) together. Add rice oil, and mix with both hands until it gets soft and stringy (you want a consistency similar to shredded cheese).

2. Add milk, and mix well. Add quinoa and bananas in pieces, and mix together.

3. Line a baking tray with a baking sheet . Divide the dough in 6 equal portions, by placing gently on the tray with a spoon. Bake for 15 minutes. Set aside and cool.

TIPS

スーパーフードといわれるキヌアを混ぜ込んで、ビタミンとミネラルをプラス。プチプチとした食感もほどよいアクセントになります。バナナは加熱するとフルクトオリゴ糖が増加し、腸内の善玉菌のえさになり、腸内環境改善にも。

Quinoa is a super food, that packs tons of vitamins and minerals, and adds an interesting crunchy accent. Bananas for sweetness is a great trick to cut down sugar not only for scones and cake, but for all your baking.

甘さ控えめで軽い食事代わりにも。
ザクザク食感と香ばしさがクセになります。

CHICKPEA OATMEAL COOKIES

These cookies make for a light, crunchy snack food that are just sweet enough without being too sugary. The oatmeal helps to fill you up so you're not snacking all day (even though you'll want to!).

ひよこ豆のオートミールクッキー

材料

約8個分

オートミール …… 50g

A
- ひよこ豆（水煮缶） …… 110g
- ピーナッツバター（無糖） …… 大さじ2
- 水 …… 大さじ2
- はちみつ …… 大さじ1
- ベーキングパウダー …… 小さじ1/2

作り方

1. オーブンを180℃に予熱する。
フードプロセッサーにAを入れ、クリーム状になるまで攪拌する。かたければ水を小さじ1くらいずつ足して調整する。ボウルに取り出し、オートミールを加えて混ぜる。

2. 手を水でぬらし、(1)を直径2cmほどに丸め、オーブンシートを敷いた天板の上に並べる。水でぬらしたフォークの背で押しつぶす。

3. オーブンで13分焼き、天板ごと取り出して冷ます。

INGREDIENTS

FOR EIGHT PIECES

Oatmeal …… 50g

A
- Chickpeas, rinsed and drained …… 110g
- Sugar-free peanut butter …… 2 tablespoons
- Water …… 2 tablespoons
- Honey …… 1 tablespoon
- Baking powder …… 1/2 teaspoon

HOW TO MAKE

1. Pre-heat the oven to 180°C.
Put all ingredients of (A) in a food processor, and process until they are creamed. If the mixture is hard, add a teaspoon of water. Set aside to a bowl, add oatmeal and mix well.

2. Soak your hands, and roll the dough into 2cm sized balls. Place on a baking tray with baking paper, evenly spaced apart. Flatten slightly with the back of a fork.

3. Bake for 13 minutes until lightly golden. Remove from the oven and allow to cool completely before removing cookies from the baking tray.

TIPS

植物性たんぱく質を多くふくむひよこ豆を使った、しっとりソフトなプロテインクッキー。食物繊維や鉄分が豊富なオートミールは、血糖値の乱高下をまねきにくく、食べごたえもあるので、朝食やトレーニング前後の補食としてもおすすめ。

Chickpeas help to add protein and keep the cookies from hardening up too much. Oatmeal adds fiber and iron, as well as volume to make these extra filling. I recommend these for a quick morning bite, or post-training snack. Make sure to let them cool thoroughly before moving!

RAINBOW SHIRATAMA

Adding vegetable paste to traditional Shiratama creates a colorful desert that has more nutrition than typical Japanese sweets. You can use these in a lot of ways with cider for a little refreshment, cr red bean paste for a traditional Japanese flavor.

野菜の自然な色合いがかわいいデザート。
いつものあんこやきな粉のほかに
サイダーに浮かべる新しい食べ方も。

カラフル白玉

材料

2人分（約16個分）

白玉粉 …… 40g
牛乳 …… 小さじ4
ほうれん草ペースト …… 10g
ビーツペースト …… 10g

野菜ペースト（作りやすい分量）

ほうれん草ペースト

ほうれん草（蒸し煮したもの。37ページ参照）25gはざく切りにし、牛乳25mlとともにフードプロセッサーにかけてペースト状にする。

ビーツペースト

ビーツ（水煮）10gは牛乳25mlとともにフードプロセッサーにかけてペースト状にする。

INGREDIENTS

FOR TWO (16 BALLS)

Shiratama powder …… 40g
Milk …… 4 teaspoons
Spinach paste …… 10g
Beetroot paste …… 10g

Spinach paste

Chop 25g of steamed spinach. Make a paste with 25ml of milk in a food processor.

Beetroot paste

Put 10g of steamed beetroots and 25ml of milk into a food processor, and make a paste.

作り方

1. ボウルに白玉粉、牛乳のそれぞれ半量とほうれん草ペーストを入れてよく混ぜる。残りも同様にビーツペーストを加えて混ぜる（ゆるければ白玉粉、かたければ牛乳を加え、耳たぶくらいのかたさにする）。

2. 鍋に湯を沸かし、(1)をひと口大に丸めながら入れ、浮いてくるまで3分ほどゆで、氷水にとって冷やす。

HOW TO MAKE

1. In a large bowl, add 20g of shiratama powder and 2 teaspoons of spinach paste. Mix the rest of shiratama powder and milk with beetroot paste. Add powder if it is too loose, and add milk if it is too hard –the mixture should be soft like your earlobe.

2. Boil water in a pan, and roll (1) as tablespoon-sized balls, and boil for 3 minutes. Set aside and cool in iced water.

TIPS

ほうれん草やビーツに多くふくまれる鉄分（吸収率の悪い非ヘム鉄）は、牛乳などの動物性食品と合わせることで吸収率もアップ。牛乳でカルシウムもとれるうえに、食感ももっちり仕上がります。大人も子どもも、一緒に丸めて楽しんで。

Shiratama is a traditional Japanese desert topping that is typically mixed with “anko” red bean paste, or “anmitsu” which is a brown sugar syrup. The milk is the key to making these soft and chewy, like mochi rice-cakes. You can adjust the amount of vegetable paste to change the flavor and depth of color.

COFFEE BREAK

うちの味噌汁

食卓の名脇役、お味噌汁。もともとは、汁ものがあるとなんだか落ち着くという夫の好みから始まったこのお味噌汁習慣もGOOD HABITを知るうえで欠かせません。
出汁は煮干しを使っています。カルシウムなどの栄養素がぎっしり詰まった煮干しは、フードプロセッサーで丸ごと粉末状にしてストック。お水にティースプーン１杯分の粉末を、パラリとふり入れるだけで、良いお出汁を味わえるのはもちろん、お椀の底の出し殻まで余すことなく楽しめるのです。
お決まりの具材は、きのこ。煮干しに多くふくまれるカルシウムは、きのこのビタミンDによって吸収率が高まるのでおすすめ。あとは野菜に豆腐に海藻に…その日の気分で3〜4種類入れています。野菜から溶け出す水溶性ビタミンも逃がさずとれます。
そして、お味噌。わが家はずっと、醸造所から取り寄せている米味噌です。原材料は米・大豆・食塩のみを使用し、その自然な甘みと出汁との相性は格別。口いっぱいに幸せが広がります。
この一杯で「あぁ帰ってきた」と心も体もほっとする、そんなお味噌汁はいかがでしょう。

MY GUIDE TO MISO SOUP

Miso soup is one of the staples of the Japanese dinner table. While I originally made miso soup because my husband liked it (having a bit of soup with his meal helps him relax), after researching healthy eating habits, it's become a must-have part of our household's GOOD HABITs.
I start with a “dashi” broth made from dried sardines. I take “Niboshi” dried sardines, which are packed with nutrients such as calcium, and grind them to a fine powder in a food processor. This powder can be stocked for a long time, and by adding just a teaspoon to some water you get a delicious soup base that you can enjoy without leftover bones or shells at the bottom of your bowl.
Since the sardines are so full of calcium, you'll also need something high in Vitamin D, which promotes calcium absorption. I highly recommend mushrooms for this task, as they contribute a distinct flavor along with their high Vitamin D content. After that, I include three to four ingredients such as tofu, seaweed, or vegetables, depending on how I'm feeling that day or what I have in stock. In the soup you'll also be able to capture all the water-soluble vitamins from your vegetables, which is a nutritional plus.
Lastly, there's the miso. In our house we always use rice miso ordered directly from the miso brewery. The only ingredients used are rice, soy beans, and salt, giving a natural sweetness that goes great with our broth, and spreads pleasantly throughout your mouth.
This one cup of soup carries all the warmth and relaxation of finally coming home after a long day. Why not try including it to add a little emotional impact to your meals as well?

GOOD HABIT

PEOPLE

上野由岐子／金正奎／大迫あゆみ／国枝愛

トップアスリートとして結果を残す表舞台の裏側には、年月をかけて積み重なる、その人らしいGOOD HABITがきっとあるはず。そんな思いから、アスリートご本人と、アスリートを支えるご家族に、食習慣にフォーカスしてお話を聞いてみました。
彼らがどんなGOOD HABITを持ち、どうやってそこにたどり着いたのか、そのプロセスにもたくさんのヒントがありました。

Behind every top athlete's performance in the public eye are months and years of steadily accumulating GOOD HABITs. With that in mind, I reached out to some professional athletes and the families that support them to find out what nutrition and lifestyle habits they use to perform at their peak.
What does a GOOD HABIT look like to them? Their answers, and the journey they took to find them, are sure to be helpful to all of us as well.

YUKIKO UENO

SHOKEI KIN

AYUMI OSAKO

AI KUNIEDA

GOOD HABIT PEOPLE

NUMBER 1

Bic Camera Takasaki BEE QUEEN

PROFILE

ソフトボール日本代表。小学校3年生からソフトボールを始め、ピッチャーとして活躍。小学校で県大会優勝、中学校で全国制覇。高校2年のとき、最年少で参加した1999年世界ジュニア選手権でエースとして優勝に貢献。卒業後、日立高崎ソフトボール部（現ビックカメラ女子ソフトボール高崎）入部。実業団入りと同時に日本代表チームにも招集され、2004年アテネオリンピックでは銅メダル、2008年北京オリンピックでは金メダルを獲得。北京オリンピックでの準決勝、決勝進出決定戦、決勝戦3試合で413球を投げきり、金メダルに大きく貢献。その活躍ぶりは「上野の413球」として語り継がれている。2020年現在まで日本代表選手であり続けると同時に、所属チームではピッチングコーチ兼選手として活躍中。

上野由岐子

YUKIKO UENO

アテネでの失敗。
それが食事の大切さを
気づかせてくれた。

——マウンドでの力強いピッチングが印象的な上野選手ですが、もともと体が丈夫なお子さんだったのですか？

実は小さいころはヒョロヒョロで、高校生までは親が作ってくれたものをただなんとなく食べているだけでしたね。食べることにもそれほど興味はなくて……。朝はギリギリまで寝ていて、母におにぎりを持たせてもらって学校へ行ったり。もちろん自分で料理を作るといったこともありませんでした。実業団に入ってからは寮生活で、ここでも出されたものを食べる毎日でした。自分で料理をするようになったのは、ひとり暮らしを始めてからなので、ここ10年くらいでしょうか。今だって、料理といっても、肉や魚を焼くとか、野菜を炒めるとか蒸すとか、手の込んだものは作りませんよ。

——食事の大切さに気づいたのはいつごろで、何がきっかけだったのですか？

アテネオリンピックのときですね。今でも時折思い出すのですが、実はあのとき、試合の前に胃腸炎にかかってしまい、チームに迷惑をかけてしまったんです。自分も納得のいくパフォーマンスができなかった。そこで、コンディショニングのための食事についても自分で考え、自分の体をコントロールできるようになろうと思ったのが最初のきっかけでした。

日々の食事で育まれた自信が
ベストパフォーマンスを後押しする。

――まずは、どんなことから変えていったのでしょう？

それまでは本当に食に無頓着だったので、栄養のことはもちろん何も知りませんでした。今でこそ積極的に取り入れている緑黄色野菜も、どれ？というレベル。幸い母が看護師をしていたので、食事に関してアドバイスをもらったり、ときに相談したりしながら、少しずつ体に良い食材や組み合わせ方を覚えていった感じです。遠征時には、食事はホテルのバイキングだったり外食だったり、ある意味食べたいものが食べたいだけある環境にあります。そこでも例えば、たんぱく質２種類を肉と大豆製品からとろう、食事には温野菜を添えようなど、「何を選んでどんなふうに食べるか」を考えるようになりました。アテネ後から次の北京オリンピックまでの期間は、アメリカに勝つことができないと金メダルの可能性はないと思っていたこともあり、正直かなりストイックに、競技とも食事とも向き合っていました。

自分の体を信じることが、自信につながる。

――ソフトボール選手として、どんな体を目指して食生活の改善をしてきたのですか？

ソフトボールというスポーツは、ボクシングのような体重制限もなければ、ラグビーのようにコンタクトスポーツでもありません。ですから、筋肉で自分の身を守らなくてはならないということはないのですが、ある程度どっしりしていないと力負けしてしまう。とはいっても、やはり軽い方が動きのスピードを上げることができますよね。ポジションごとに求められるパフォーマンスが違い、さらに同じピッチャーというポジション内でもいろいろなタイプがいます。私を例にあげると、あまりに軽すぎると重いボールが投げられなくなるので、ある程度のウエイトは欲しい。理想は、必要な筋肉はつけつつ、やわらかさもある状態。つまり、適度に脂肪もあって体力・持久力が持続する体の方が良いと考えています。ソフトボールという競技だからこういう体になろうという決まった型ではなく、私自身に合ったのがこういう体だと思っています。食事については、カロリーなど細かい数字はそれほど重視していません。だけど、あらかじめ栄養の基本を知ったうえで、きちんと食べるということが、自分の自信につながって、大事な場面を前に背中を押してくれることがある。考えてとる食事の意味はここにあると思います。実際には、食事でパフォーマンスがどう変わったか、ほかのスポーツに比べてわかりにくい競技でもあるんですよ。なぜなら、試合中に守備と攻撃が交互にあって、座っている時間も作れるから。それより、昨日はこういう食事で準備をして、今日はこういう食事で疲労回復をしたから、きっと大丈夫っていう安心感の方が大きい。自分の体を信頼できれば、パフォーマンスの強さや自信につながります。

ただ30歳をこえて、食生活は変わっていないのに、脂肪のつき方や体のキレが変わったことを体感してしまったときは衝撃的で……。年相応に、何でおなかを満たすかを考えていかないとだめだなっていうのは思うようになりました。

今の自分にとって大切な要素は、安心感や心地よさ

――30歳で訪れるその変化、とてもよくわかります。ところで、毎日どんな食事をされているのですか？

朝はフルーツ、グラノーラとヨーグルトで軽めにすることが多いですね。あとバナナが好きなのでよく食べます。昼はグラウンドでお弁当をとるんですが、12時には食べ始めるため、あまり朝からガッツリ食べてしまうと消化しきれない感じもあって。

夜は家に帰って自分で作りますが、今日肉を食べたら明日は魚とか、何を作るか迷わないようにしているくらいです。あとはそのときの体調に合わせて、鉄をとるならこの食材で、吸収率を上げられるこのビタミンを合わせようといった工夫をしています。練習や試合内容によっては、今日は2イニングしか投げなかったからあまり炭水化物をとらなくていいなといった量の調節や、多く投げた日は消化が良くて高たんぱくなメニューを合わせようとか。疲れているときは、食べやすい薄切りの肉を選んだり……。おもに筋疲労からの回復を考えていますね。

野菜は緑黄色野菜のほか、キャベツをよく食べます。群馬は野菜、特にキャベツがおいしいのでおすすめです！せん切りにして生でも炒めてもおいしいし、塩昆布と合わせた浅漬けもよく作ります。あとは薄切り肉と合わせてレンジでチンしてポン酢しょうゆで食べたり。

ちなみに食事のひと口めは汁もので胃をあたためて、野菜から先に食べています。そのちょっとした心づかいで気持ちが満たされたり、心地よさを感じるんです。

――気持ちよく続けることが大切ですよね。ここぞ！というときの食事のルーティーンはありますか？

基本、ありませんね。あまりルーティーンにこだわりたくないんです。要はどういう環境でも、どういう状況でも、ベストパフォーマンスができるようにしたい。突然、30分後試合だよって言われても、そこでベストが出せる強い自分でいたいんですよ。ソフトボールって外競技で雨が降っても強行したり、海外に行くと試合時間が直前に変わったりすることもしばしば。だからふだんからしっかりと食事をとり、臨機応変に、何でも受け入れられるということを大事にしています。

ただ、試合当日は腹持ちのする、消化がゆっくりなものを食べるようにしています。ピッチャーは拘束時間が長いぶん、体力も集中力もたくさん消費します。おなかがすいてしまうことで、余計なところに集中力を使いたくないんですよね。バッターと対峙しているそのときに100％のパフォーマンスをしたいんです。昔から試合前はおにぎりを食べることが多いかな。シンプルな塩むすびか、具は鮭や昆布が好き。明太子は苦手なんです、福岡出身なのに…！

それから、絶対試合前には食べないものがひとつあります。

――なんでしょう？

納豆です。試合前の朝食に納豆を食べた日は、9割ぐらい負けてるんです。それに気づいてからは、納豆を食べないというのがルーティーンかもしれないです。ジンクスですね。大好きなので夜は食べますよ。

食べるものすべてが自分の身に。このことを忘れないでほしい。

――これからアスリートを目指す若い人たちに、アドバイスをするとしたら？

食事に関しては、口にするものはすべて、必ず自分の身になるということを忘れないでほしいですね。好きなものを食べることまで無理して我慢することはないと思うんです。私もたまには心の栄養、なんて言ってチョコレートなどお菓子を食べることももちろんあります。でも昨日お菓子を食べたから、今日はダッシュをプラス３本しようなどと考える。体への影響を意識して食べると、そのあとの行動が変わるんですよね。知っていて食べるのと、ただなんとなく好きだから食べるのでは、体へのつき方や次の練習への意欲が変わるんです。ポテトチップス１枚にしてもそう。体に良くないから食べてはいけないという強制的なものではなくて、自分自身が選んで食べるものに責任を持っていてほしいなと思います。

まだまだ、投げられるうちは現役を続けていきたいと思っているので、これからも日々の積み重ねを意識していきたいです。また将来的に指導者になったとき、それを後輩たちに伝えられるようになりたいと思っています。ずばり言うならば、「いつもの食事に緑黄色野菜を加える」「たんぱく質は２種類とる」「試合や体の調子に応じて、炭水化物の量を加減する」かな。技術を教えてくれる人はたくさんいるし、それも大事だけれど、アスリートは自分の体を知り、上手に操っていくことが大切ですから。

RECIPE

鶏手羽元のさっぱり煮

材料

作りやすい分量

鶏手羽元		10本
A	酢	1/2カップ
	しょうゆ／みりん／水	各1/4カップ
	砂糖	大さじ1
	おろししょうが	適量
サラダ油		少々

作り方

1. フライパンにサラダ油を中火で熱し、手羽先を入れ、表面がこんがりするまで焼く。
2. 圧力鍋に移し、Aを加えてふたをし、強火にかける。
3. 圧力がかかったら火を止め、自然に圧力が下がるまでおく。

TIPS

「スーパーでお手頃な鶏手羽元を見つけたときによく作ります。まとめて作っておくと食事づくりも楽になります。実は酢の酸味が苦手なのですが、これは酸味が飛んでさっぱりとした味わいになるので、おいしいですよ。圧力鍋だと短時間でできるし、骨離れもよく煮上がります。私は脂っこい皮は除いてしまいますが、皮ごと食べてももちろんOKです。」

YUKIKO UENO

GOOD HABIT PEOPLE

NUMBER 2

PROFILE

プロラグビープレーヤー。トップリーグ・NTTコミュニケーションズシャイニングアークス主将。小学生時代は水泳、バスケットをやっていたが、中学時代に母のすすめ、兄の影響でラグビーを始める。高校時代に全国大会優勝、早稲田大学では2度の全国大会準優勝経験を持つ。卒業後、NTTコミュニケーションズシャイニングアークスに加入。2016年に主将となり、同年日本代表に選出される。日本代表キャップは7。アスリートとしての食習慣の大切さに気づき、「#きんめし」として栄養を意識した食生活について発信し、多くのフォロワーに支持されている。
twitter／instagram: @shokei1003

金正奎

SHOKEI KIN

食事と体がリンクしたとき一生続けたいという確信に変わった。

——「きんめし」をはじめ現役アスリートの食習慣をリードしている金選手ですが、小さいころはどんなお子さんだったのでしょう？

小さいころはおなかいっぱい肉とごはんばかり食べていましたね。実家が焼肉屋で、焼肉が大好き。それこそファストフードも揚げものも好きで、実は小学校の4年生くらいまではかなり太っていたんです。地元・大阪で身近なお好み焼きなどいわゆる粉もんもよく食べました。ラグビーを始めてからも、高校3年までは実家にいましたが、料理することはゼロ、食事の質や内容は意識したこともなかったです。正確に言うと、その後大学に入ってもしばらくはそんな感じでした。

——食に対する意識が変わったきっかけはありましたか？また変化を実感できたのはどんなときだったのでしょう？

大学2年のときにパーソナルトレーナーについてトレーニングをするようになり、トレーニングをがんばっているなら、食事もがんばりたいという意識に変わったんです。最初はトレーナーの教えをそのまま実践して。そこから、自分に合うものを体の反応と照らし合わせていく中で見つけていきました。

食生活の改善を始めたころは、正直言って大変で。それこそ好きだったファストフードや揚げものもNG。本当にこれで体が変わるのか、意味があるのかと半信半疑で、かなり葛藤しながらやっていました。

いい食事、いいトレーニング、いい睡眠。
これがここ一番というときのキレを生む。

実際に変化を実感したのは、大学4年から社会人になったくらいでしょうか。何より自分の思うように体が動くようになった。ここでしっかり動き出したいという場面で動けるようになっていたり、疲れにくくなったり。タフなトレーニング後も、明らかに他の選手よりもリカバリーのスピードが速い。食事って本当に大事だと気づかされた瞬間でした。それからは揚げものを食べないとか、たんぱく質も魚や鶏肉中心にしたり、得た知識に確信を持って実践できるようになりました。当時は大きく制限がかかっているように思えたことも、今では当たりまえの習慣になっています。

自分との相性の良い食事が、未来のための土台を作る。

――体が変わるまでには時間がかかりますよね。具体的には、どんなことに気をつけているのですか？

大事なのでくり返しますが、自分の体の感覚を尊重するようにしています。自分に合うもの合わないものを感じ取って、取捨選択するということでしょうか。体のキレに不要なものはとりたくない、それにつながるのが余分な油であれば揚げものは控えたり、魚の脂は熱を通さないほうが体内で効率よく利用できると聞いたら実際に試してみて、体の反応も良ければ焼くより刺身で食べたり。食べ順でいうと、カーボラスト。たんぱく質を先に食べ、ごはんが最後に残るようにしています。試合前は、内臓にかかるダメージのリスクを避けるために、生ものには気をつけています。そういったことのくり返しを、日々続けています。

実は食事の内容だけでなく、食べる時間にもこだわっていて。朝はだいたい6時、昼は練習時間にもよりますが12時くらい、夜は5時か5時半ごろには食べます。早めに夕飯を食べるのには理由があって、たくさん食べるぶん、とる時間が遅いだけ満腹感が夜中まで続いてしまいます。そのまま寝てしまうと、良い睡眠がとれないんです。夜中にトイレで起きてしまうこともありますし。そこで食事時間を早めたところ、寝るまでには食べたものはしっかり消化され、夜はぐっすり眠れて、朝はおなかがすいて目が覚めたんです。これが自分にとっては幸せなことで、1日のいいスタートが切れると気づきました。仕事や環境によってできない人も多いと思いますが、いつもよりちょっと早めに食べるということを試してみてもいいかもしれません。

――夕食の時間、今日から早めてみます！ところで、金選手はどのような体を目指してトレーニングや良い食習慣を心がけていますか？

もちろんラグビーは大きい選手が多いですけど、大きければいいかというとそうではない。僕なんかは小さい方ですが、トップリーグの選手を続けられているのは、自分の体をしっかり自分で扱えているから。動かしたいように動かせているからなんです。たとえば体重が100kgあって、自分の体を80％コントロールできる人と、90kgで100％コントロールできる人がいたとしたら、後者の方が、ラグビーに限らずどの競技でも良いパフォーマンスが発揮できると思います。理想の体って、見た目じゃなくて、体の感覚じゃないかと。この動きの感覚の誤差をいかになくせるか。そのためには食事も大事、トレーニングも大事、睡眠も大事。僕の中では、この中のどれかひとつがかけてもだめなんです。

以前大きなけがをしたときも、治るまで1年くらいかかると言われていたところ、実際には3カ月ほどで完治し、復帰することができました。自分の体への反応が良い食材をしっかりとって、十分な睡眠もとって、リハビリに励む。このサイクルを続けてきたおかげだと思います。あらかじめ体に合うものを知っていて、ベースが整っていたことも大きいですね。これは復帰スピードだけでなく、競技力の向上にもつながるかと。近年の自分は年を重ねても衰えはなく、むしろ集中力・持久力が伸びているように感じています。

魚が8割。肉2割。
これが今の僕の体に
一番合った食事。

――ふだんの食事はどうされてるのですか？

練習がある日の昼はチームの食事があるので、朝と夜を家で食べます。朝はほぼ決まったものを。オートミールに無脂肪のヨーグルト、あとはカットフルーツを加えてます。夜は魚がメインの食事が8割ですね。あとは鶏肉。このバランスが今の僕の体には一番合っているんです。

結婚してからは夕食の多くを妻が作ってくれます。いつも6〜7品のおかずを用意し、いろいろな食材からまんべんなく栄養がとれるように工夫されていて感謝してます。妻のチキン南蛮は絶品！もちろん肉は揚げずに、タルタルソースもマヨネーズを使わずに豆乳で仕上げてくれて、それが出てきた日は、ヨッシャ！って。

社会人になってから始めた料理も年々作る頻度は上がっています。食事を突き詰めていく中で、自分で作ることを通じてさらに気づきを得たいと思って。さばなど青魚系が好きで、水煮のさば缶やいわし缶をよく使いますね。扱いやすくて、アレンジもしやすいので1日1缶は食べているかも。いわし缶のパスタは試合前にも食べる僕の得意料理のひとつです。長く続けられる食事には手軽さも大事だと気づかされました。

ときには外食もします。漁港の町に住んでいるので、魚料理が自慢の店がたくさんあります。常連になって、少し塩分を控えめにと協力をしてもらうことも。そういうことができるのは本当にありがたいですね。千葉にはおいしい鮮魚店も多いんですよ。

――ご自身の食スタイルが、まわりの人に影響を与えたということはありますか？

ラグビーの仲間が食事について相談してくれたり、魚を食べる人が増えているような気がしますが……。もしかすると妻が一番変わったかもしれません。一緒の食事をしてきて、便秘が治ったり、むくみがなくなったり、健康になったと言ってました。彼女はアスリートではありませんが、体に良い影響が出ているようです。

自分に正直に向き合う、
そして問いかけ続けよう。

――食生活を改善したいと考え始めている選手や、未来のアスリートに向けて、アドバイスをお願いします。

やはり体を作るベースとなる、「たんぱく質をいろいろな種類からとる」ことは大事だと思います。魚や鶏肉、納豆などをバランスよく。何事もかたよるのは良くないですよ。最近はジュニア世代でもプロテイン飲んでますとか、子どもたちにどんなプロテインを与えたらいいですかといった質問をいただくこともあります。これについてはちょっと違うなと感じることもあって、「たくさん咀嚼すること」も僕は大事だと考えています。あごの筋力を衰えさせることは競技力の低下にもつながります。ほかにも咀嚼は脳が活性化したり、メリットがとても多いと思います。

少々極端な話をしてしまうと、子ども時代は何を食べたっていいんです。毎日親が作ってくれた料理は好き嫌いせず、よく噛んで残さず食べる、その方が大事です。そしてできれば、「夕食は18時までに終わらせる」こと。睡眠の質を高めることと消化器系のトラブルを防ぐこと、どちらにも効果的。あとは何を食べるにしても、自分の体に常に問いかけてみてほしい。自分にとって良いのか、そうでないのか。そういうアンテナが張れる人は、必ずプラスの方向に働きかけられると思うんです。

最後に、「続けること」。食事を変えたことによる結果は、すぐに伴わないかもしれません。ですが、自分に合ったこの習慣をずっと大事にすることで、自分の人生ももっと豊かになる、そう信じてます。

RECIPE

たことさば缶の
ガーリックトマト煮

材料

2人分

ゆでだこ	150g
さば水煮缶	1缶(190g)
ホールトマト缶	1缶(400g)
にんにく(つぶす)	1片
オリーブ油	大さじ2
塩／こしょう／ドライバジル	各少々

作り方

1. たこはひと口大に切る。
2. 鍋にオリーブ油を弱火で熱し、にんにくを炒める。香りが出たらたこ、ホールトマトをつぶしながら加え、中火でひと煮立ちさせたら、さば缶を缶汁ごと加える。
3. 塩、こしょうで調味し、弱火で10分ほど煮る。器に盛り、バジルをちらす。

TIPS

「さば水煮缶もたこもよく登場する食材。大好きなんです！そのふたつをひと皿でとれる最強のレシピを考えてみました。何よりたんぱく質がしっかりとれて、栄養価が高い。何か野菜を加えたり、パスタにアレンジしてもおいしいと思います。」

SHOKEI KIN

GOOD HABIT PEOPLE

NUMBER 3

Kumasaka Photography

PROFILE

夫は陸上長距離種目の大迫傑選手。2015年よりアメリカ・オレゴン州ポートランド在住。2人の子どもを育てながら、大迫選手の競技生活を支えている。トップアスリートの妻として、セミナー、講演会への登壇も。オレゴンでの日々を綴るSNSも人気。Instagram: @ayu_sako

大迫 傑 選手

プロマラソンランナー。ナイキ所属。3000m、5000mの日本記録を保持。2020年の東京マラソンでは、2時間5分29秒の日本新記録で日本人トップの4位入賞。その結果、東京オリンピックのマラソン日本代表に選出された。オリンピック、世界選手権など世界大会での活躍に注目が集まっている。

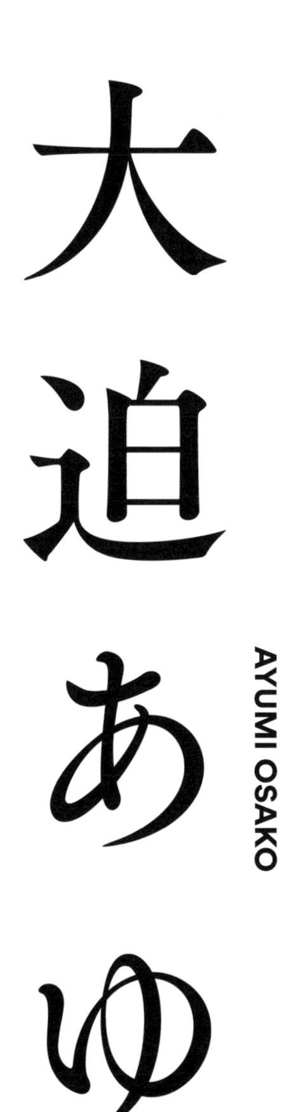

マラソンを走るように
ゆったりと
心に余裕を持ちながら。

自分も本気で走ったあの日から
ランナーの気持ちに近づいた。

――大迫家の具体的な食事の内容を教えてください。

基本的には、夫の体調によって準備する食事内容を工夫しています。朝起きたときの胃腸の調子や、午前中の練習終了時の内臓疲労度は日によって違うので、固形物を摂取するのが辛いときはスムージーやコールドプレスジュースを利用することも多いのです。ジュースに使えそうな、いちごや桃、マンゴー、パイナップル、ブルーベリーなどのフルーツや、ケールはいつも冷蔵庫に常備するようにしています。夏場はスイカもよく食べていますね。

夜はいろいろとおかずを作り置きして、気に入ったものがあればバイキングのように好きなものを好きなだけ食べられるようにはしています。練習が終わった時点での「今日はガッツリ食べられそう」「今日はちょっと疲れた」といった言葉を聞き逃さないようにして、たくさん作ったり、消化の良いものにしたりなど、夫のリクエストや体調に合わせて作ります。なので、買い出しも毎日行きます。

１年の半分以上は合宿だったりと家を空けることも多いのですが、一緒に過ごせる間は家族みんなで食卓を囲む時間を大切にしています。たまに夫みずから豚のしょうが焼きを作ることもあるんですよ。

――育児と両立しながら食事のサポートをされているあゆみさん、料理はもともと得意だったのですか？

学生時代はひとり暮らしをしていましたが、実は炊飯器でごはんを炊くのもおぼつかないくらいでした。料理は夫と結婚してからのゼロスタートです。夫の母が段取りよくおいしい料理を作る方なので、今も帰国時には大迫家秘伝のもんじゃ焼きや南蛮漬けや餃子など、家庭の味をいろいろ教えてもらっています。栄養のことも、何もわからないところから覚えていきました。

忙しいときや今すぐ栄養を補強したいときは、無理して作ることはせず、お味噌汁のインスタント食品や缶詰、乾物も利用します。もちろん、デリバリーも頼みますし、外食からは新しい味つけのヒントがもらえると、夫も楽しんでくれています。

――食事での失敗談などはありますか？またそれをどう乗り越えましたか？

最初のころのことですが、張りきって食事の準備をしたのに、どうも夫はそういう食事がとれる調子ではなかったようで、あまり食べてくれず、くやしい思いをすることもありました。

そこで、私も走ってみたんです！実際に走ってみたら、ランナーの気持ちがわかるかなって。トレーニングをして、大会にエントリーもしました。もちろん夫のレベルとは全然違いますが。するとたしかに、きつい練習のあとではそんなには食べられないし、むしろジャンクなものが食べたくなったりという気持ちもそのときに納得感を持って理解できたんです。そこから、だんだん寄り添えるようなってきたかな。

転機はマラソンへの転向、そしてあの日本新記録まで。

――食事の大切さに気づいたのは、何かきっかけがあったのですか？

ターニングポイントは2回ありました。1回目は夫が20代前半のころ。当時の夫は、太りたくないという理由で、たんぱく源となる肉ばかりを食べていたり、ときにはエネルギーもたんぱく質もとれるとアイスだけで食事を済ませる、そんなこともありました。まだ若いからこそどうにか保てていた部分があったと思うのですが、これを5年、10年続けていては、おそらく世界で戦える体には仕上がらないよねと考えたタイミングです。

2回目は、5km、10kmなどのトラック競技から、40km以上走るマラソンに転向することになったとき。トラックの何倍も走るわけですから、今までと同じ内容ではエネルギーが足りない、食事から変えていこうという話になったんです。そのときは夫が20代半ばを過ぎたころで、変化にも前向きでした。

――実際に食事を変えてみて、あゆみさんから見て、大迫選手の変化を実感したことはありますか？

当時、夫が所属していたナイキオレゴンプロジェクトは、オリンピックなどの世界大会で金メダル、銀メダルを取れるレベルのチームメイトばかりで、最初は試合に出ても勝負をさせてもらえない状況でした。それが、少しずつそうした選手の背中に追いついていき、2018年にはシカゴマラソンでチームメイトを追い越して1度目の日本新記録更新、そして2020年には2度目の日本新記録を更新することができました。年々成績が上向き、結果がついてきているのが実感かなと思います。

――大迫選手は食事について、どうお考えなのでしょうか？

大事なパートのひとつということは理解していますが、食事に生活を左右されたくないとは言っています。人によって合うスタイルはそれぞれで、正解はありません。ですが、管理された食事をとることで、安心感よりプレッシャーになってしまうのは私も避けたいと思っていて。きっちり管理することが自信につながる選手もいるはずですが、夫の場合は、ある程度の余白を持って臨機応変に対応する方が良さそうです。栄養の話も、本人から聞かれない限りは私からもしません。たとえレースでの結果が良くなかったときでも、気をつかって食事内容を変えられる方が夫にはプレッシャーのようなので、なるべくいつもと変わらない食事を作ります。私たちは何年も連れ添ってきて、こうあるべきという型にとらわれずに、自由に、状況を楽しみながら対応していくことに、新たな発見や学びがあると思うようになりました。

どんな環境もみんなで楽しむ、
これが毎日快適に過ごす秘訣。

――オレゴンといえば豊かな自然と住みやすい街のイメージがありますが、海外での生活で大変なことはありますか？

もうこちらに来て5年になりましたが、何を買っても大容量で、使いきれないというストレスはありますね。それから和食を作ろうと思うと、乾物も調味料も缶詰も手には入るのですが、日本の倍くらいの値段はするかもしれません。そういったこともあり、最近はおくらやみょうが、ねぎ、大葉など、使いたい野菜を家庭菜園で育てるようになりました。一方では、ファーマーズマーケットに行けば地元でとれた新鮮な有機野菜が買えたり、季節ごとのフルーツは日本より充実しているかもしれません。オレゴンでは、畑に出かけて、旬のフルーツを自分たちの好きなだけ収穫ができるU-Pickというのも盛んで、家族みんなでたくさん摘んできたブルーベリーを小分けにして冷凍庫にストックしておき、スムージーとして食べたりしています。

――マラソン選手ならではの食事の工夫はありますか？またトレーニング期とレース前で食事内容を変えることはありますか？

長距離はガス欠を起こさないようにすることが大切なので、エネルギー源となる炭水化物をしっかりとれるようにと考えました。夫は、炭水化物は体が重くなると抵抗があったようでしたが、ごはんのすすむ丼ものを多くしたり、汁ものにとろみをつけるなど、自然にとれるように工夫したんです。

また、スープや味噌汁は日頃からよく取り入れていて、汗をかき続けたあとの水分補給に加え、溶け出した栄養も余すことなくとれ、さらに体をあたためて内臓の動きを良くしてくれるすぐれものです。

汁もの以外では、普段はできるだけ栄養を損なわない生の状態で食べるようにしているのですが、大会前は火を通すことが多いです。中でも特に食物繊維に気をつかっています。走っているときにおなかの調子が悪くなったり脇腹が痛くなったりすることを避けるため、食物繊維の多い食材はホロホロになるまで煮くずす工夫をしています。

レース後は、最低限の回復食をとったあとは、本人が食べたいごほうび優先。ときには一緒にお酒を楽しんだり、実は夫はクリームの乗ったケーキや甘いものも好きなんですよ。

受け継いできた習慣と今の自分に合った習慣をともに。

――ずっと続けている勝負飯はありますか？

大会前は必ずうなぎを食べてます。夫が中学生くらいから続けている習慣のようで、どんなに地方の大会でもうなぎ屋さんを探しに行きます。海外では、日本食スーパーで手に入れて。値段は日本の倍くらいしますけどね。レース前に脂質の高いものを食べることはあまり推奨されていないのかもしれませんが、大会前日にゲン担ぎとして食べることが多いです。レース直前はカステラ。これも昔からずっと続けていて、胃もたれなくすぐエネルギーになるように、バターなど脂質が少ないシンプルなものを選んで食べています。夫の昔からのルーティーンも大切にすることが、レースに向けた心の準備につながっているのではないでしょうか。

――最後に、ご家族みんなで楽しく続けられるアイデアをぜひ教えてください。

ひとつは「体の中にレインボー」。娘にもわかりやすい表現で、色とりどりにいろんな食材をとろうということです。もうひとつは、「晴れた日はビタミン。疲れた日はお酢」。ランナーは基本屋外で日を浴びて活動しているので、紫外線や活性酸素の害を取りのぞく意味でビタミンをしっかりとろう、酢はエネルギーとなるグリコーゲンの生成を助けるので、疲れたときには積極的にとろうということです。これを合言葉にしています。

RECIPE

ケールとキヌアのサラダ

材料

作りやすい分量

	材料	分量
	ケール	1束
	キヌア	1カップ
	トマト	1個
	きゅうり	1本
A	白ワインビネガー	大さじ3
	オリーブ油	大さじ2
	塩／こしょう／粉チーズ／レモン汁	各適量

作り方

1. 鍋にキヌアと水２カップを入れて煮立て、ふたをして中火で15分ほど炊く。水分が少なくなってきたら弱火にし、こげないように混ぜながら水分を飛ばす。バットに広げて冷ます。
2. ケール、トマト、きゅうりは食べやすく刻む。
3. ボウルにＡを合わせ、(1)、(2)を加えてあえる。

TIPS

「たくさん作ってほぼ毎日のように食べています。ケールはビタミンＣのほか、メラトニンという成分がふくまれていて、良い睡眠がとれるとされています。歯ごたえもよく、満腹感が得やすく、食べ過ぎも防げます。キヌアはすべての必須アミノ酸のほか、さまざまな栄養がふくまれるスーパーフード。お気に入りのレストランで聞いたレシピをアレンジしました。りんごやグレープフルーツを加えてもおいしいです。」

AYUMI OSAKO

GOOD HABIT PEOPLE

NUMBER 4

PROFILE

夫はプロ車いすテニスプレーヤーの国枝慎吾選手。国枝選手とは大学時代の同級生で、2011年に結婚。2013年、アスリートフードマイスターの資格を取得。コーチ、トレーナーとともに海外遠征にも同行し、競技生活を全面的にサポートしている。SNSでは日々の食事を発信中。

twitter: @aikunieda　instagram: @ai_meshi3241

国枝慎吾 選手

日本初のプロ車いすテニスプレーヤー・世界ランキング1位。グランドスラム車いす部門で、男子世界歴代最多となる計45回（シングルス24回・ダブルス21回）優勝の記録を持つとともに、ギネス世界記録も更新中。パラスポーツ全体の普及活動のキーパーソンとしても活躍。

国枝

AI KUNIEDA

長く世界の第一線で活躍する夫と
これからも二人三脚で歩んでいきたい。

好きなのはシンプルな味つけ、無理なく継続できる方法を見つけて。

――国枝家の日ごろの食事について教えてください。

　最近では朝にコーヒーを飲むようになり、朝食はごはん食よりもパン食が多くなりました。サラダ、目玉焼きとウインナー２本、トースト、ヨーグルト、フルーツ、オレンジジュース、そしてコーヒーというのが定番メニューです。そのあと夫は必ずトレーニングや練習があるので、朝はわりとしっかり食べています。

　サラダはベビーリーフやケールなどの葉もの野菜や、薄切りにしたパプリカなどを洗って保存容器に入れ、冷蔵庫にストックしておきます。朝起きたら器に盛るだけ。あとは、ミニトマトがあればのせたり。出かけるまでの時間短縮にそうしているのですが、むしろこの保存方法にすると野菜がしゃきっとしておいしいんです。２～３日は日持ちしますよ。市販のドレッシングは使わず、体に良いといわれているアマニ油をかけています。冷蔵庫の場所は取りますが、これさえあれば手早くビタミン補給ができて安心、とても重宝してます。

　昼は夫にお弁当を持たせたり、家で一緒に食べるときは前日の残りものや焼魚などをいただきます。よく作り置きしている、野菜とツナのあえものや、なすの煮びたしなどを合わせていますね。夜はメインをその日ごとに変えて、おかずを小鉢３つ、そこにサラダや納豆を添えています。とりたい品数に合わせて使う食器もあらかじめ決めて、そのお皿を埋めていくイメージで準備するとスムーズです。

いわゆる、しょうゆ・酒・みりんはおいしいのですが多用しないように気をつけていて、シンプルなオイルや塩で味つけすることが多いです。

——どの作り置きも便利で、今日から始めたくなります。料理は昔から得意だったのですか？

私は３人姉妹の長女で、下の妹とは年が少し離れているのでよく母の手伝いをしていて。そこで教わった料理や、学校の調理実習で習ったレシピを書き写して、自分のレシピノートを作っていたんです。母は関西出身で基本は薄味、素材を生かしたシンプルな料理をよく作ってくれていました。

——そんな愛さんでもどうしても疲れて作りたくない！という日はあるのですか？

作り置きに頼れる日はいいんですが、そんな余力もない日ありますよね。そのときは外に食べに出かけたり、デリバリーを活用します。おうちでなかなかしない焼肉を食べに行くことが多いかな。夫はお肉が好きなんです。

良いものは試してみる。
合うものを長く続けていく。

——今までに何かご自身でもスポーツはされていたのですか？

それがスポーツとは無縁、実は運動も得意ではなくて。それこそ結婚するまできちんとテニスのルールもわからず、試合を見たのは数えるほど、アスリートというより学生時代の友人と結婚したという感覚でした。2009年に彼がプロになったときも、あまりピンとは来ていなかったかもしれません。

——栄養学を学んだきっかけを教えてください。そして、それまでの食事からどう変えたのでしょう？

アスリートはまさに体が資本。たとえばけがをすると体へのダメージはもちろん、収入にも直結してくるわけです。大変なことですよね。結婚した翌年、2012年に夫がロンドンパラリンピックに出場しましたが、大会直前にけがをしてしまい、手術を経験したんです。そのときは術後の経過も良く、金メダルを獲得することができたのですが、これを機に食事とパフォーマンスの関係に意識が向くようになりました。もちろん、食事でけがが治せるわけではないのですが、日々の食事次第で多少なりとも予防できるかもしれない、より良いパフォーマンスにつながるかもしれないと思って。

知識をもとにいきなり大きく生活を変えるというより、体に良いと思うものを積極的に取り入れてみて、良ければ続けて、合わないなと思ったらやめる。そういうことをくり返してきました。

——ちなみに、お家で栄養の話はされてますか？

話しますよ。夫からこういうものが体に良いって聞いたけどどうなの？って聞いてくることもあれば、こちらから伝えることも。2020年の全豪オープンのときは、試合がせまった時期のコンディショニングのひとつとして、試合前１週間ほどはカフェインを控えておき、試合直前にカフェインをとることでパフォーマンスを上げるという私が聞いた方法を夫に提案し、実践しました。新しいものも取り入れながら、常にそのときにベストなコンディションづくりを模索しています。

遠征時は食事よりも試合準備。日ごろのぶれない土台づくりに対話が欠かせない。

――車いすテニスという競技のプレーヤーならではの工夫もあるのでしょうか？

私がサポーターとしていつも大切にしているのは、本人の感覚を共有してもらうことです。車いすでテニスをする姿はとてもハードに見えますが、主に上半身を使っているのでカロリー消費は意外と少ないのです。また、車いすだと日常的に家で体脂肪率まではかることができません。だから、たとえば体を大きくしたいときは、体重の数値と本人の感覚を目安に、私はお米や芋類の準備する量を調整します。一方で、本人の体が重いという感覚は、体重そのものではなく車いすの重さや鈍さに理由があることもあります。夫はふだんの生活に関してはとても大らかですが、テニスに関することにはセッティング１ミリのズレもキャッチできるくらい敏感。日々の会話の中で体調や気になることを聞きながら私の食事内容も工夫していく感じです。

――テニスは世界各地の転戦や連戦が多いと思いますが、海外遠征時の食事についても気になります。

グランドスラムでは大会側の用意が素晴らしく、こだわりの食材があったり、キッチンがついているホテルで作ることができますが、訪れる国によっては環境も厳しく、現地でバランスよく食べるのが難しいのです。さらに本人にとって、遠征中は食事の優先順位が低くて。次の日の試合に備えて、１分でも早くホテルに帰って準備することが何より大事。体のケアだったり、対戦選手のビデオを見たり。外に食べに行って選ぶ時間も惜しいほどです。

それから大会はアメリカやヨーロッパで開催されることが多いので、移動時間がとても長い日本人には不利と言われていて。どこへ行くにも10時間、15時間かかりますので、それだけでかなり疲れが出ます。ですからいかに、日本にいる間に変化に耐えられる土台を作っておくことが大事か。食事内容を工夫し始めてから、夫もこの移動のあとのリカバリーが早くなったと言っています。

あと、遠征時に必ず持っていくものは、おにぎりを作るためのアルファ米、フリーズドライのおみそ汁、エナジーバー代わりの小さいようかんです。野菜が食べられないこともあるので、青汁も持っていきます。

――試合当日の食事はどうされているのでしょう？

テニスは試合が何時に始まるか読めないので、コンディショニングのコントロールがなかなか難しいのが現実です。当日は、自分が試合をするコートの進行具合を常に気にしておきます。試合が始まる時間にある程度予想を立てておき、それに合わせて試合準備や食事の時間をとってます。おにぎりやゼリー飲料を保冷バッグに用意して、タイミングや体調に合わせて本人が選んで補うイメージです。試合後はリカバリーのために、終了後30分以内におにぎりやサンドイッチを食べることが多いですね。

――大会前後の食事では何か特別な用意をしていますか？

大会前に変わったことや気づかいをしてしまうと、かえってプレッシャーになる気がして。いつも通りが一番だと思っています。私自身も同行するとなると、冷蔵庫の中を整理してから出発したいという作り手の事情も正直ありますし……！

大会後、日本に帰ってきたときは、1週間くらいのオフをとります。そのときは本人が好きなもの、食べたいものを食べるようにしています。おすしでもラーメンでも、好きなものを食べてリラックスしましょうって。

食事に込められた思いと工夫、夫婦でどんな逆境も乗り越えてきた。

――健康的な食事を作り続けてきて、愛さんから見て、国枝選手のここが改善したと感じることはありますか？

良くなった実感……夫は今36歳で、その年齢で世界ランキング1位として活躍できているってすごいことだと思います。もちろん本人の努力が一番大きいのですが、そこに少しでも食事が関わっているとすればうれしいなって。2016年のリオパラリンピック前の手術を機に引退を考えることもありましたが、こうやって一緒に乗り越えてきましたから。

――世界一のプロテニスプレーヤーを、一番近くで支え続ける秘訣とは何でしょう？

食事に関しては、まずは「彩りよくすること」「メインとおかずに一品ずつたんぱく質をとること」「シンプルな味つけにすること」でしょうか。

あとは毎日3食のごはんを作るのは考えるだけで大変なので、無理はしないことです。ときにはお惣菜や冷凍食品を買うことも、時間を買うと思って。心にゆとりを持って、気持ちよく過ごしていければと思っています。

RECIPE

豚バラのピリ辛丼

材料

2人分

豚バラ薄切り肉 …… 250g
長ねぎ …… 1/2本
A 白いりごま …… 大さじ1
　コチュジャン／豆板醤／はちみつ …… 各小さじ1
　ごま油 …… 少々
温かいごはん …… 適量
万能ねぎの小口切り／糸唐辛子（好みで） …… 各少々

作り方

1. 長ねぎは白髪ねぎにし、ざるに入れて10分ほどおく。
2. 豚肉はひと口大に切る。鍋に湯を沸かし、豚肉を入れて色が変わるまでゆで、水けをきる。
3. ボウルにAを合わせ、（1）、（2）を加えてあえる。ごはんにのせ、好みで万能ねぎ、糸唐辛子をのせる。

TIPS

「母がよく作ってくれた一品で私たち夫婦の大好物。豚肉のビタミンB_1と長ねぎのアリシンは疲労回復、スタミナアップに効果的。豚肉はゆでるので余分な脂も落とせます。白髪ねぎは水にさらさず、空気に触れさせることで有効成分の損失をおさえつつ、辛みを飛ばします。コチュジャンのピリ辛が食欲をそそりますよ。豆腐にのせるのもおすすめです。」

AI KUNIEDA

GOOD HABIT, GOOD DAY

GOOD HABITで良い毎日

GOOD HABITでお伝えしてきた、日常に栄養学の知識を取り入れながら、細く長く続けられるシンプルな方法やレシピ。その根っこには、私の好きな「フードは風土」という考え方があります。

「地産地消」を心がけた食材選びは、「自分が住む地域を応援すること」「風土を形づくること」「風土や文化を発展させていくこと」。さらにもっと視野を広げると、「世界に日本を誇ること」「世界の国々の食文化をたたえること」にもつながっていくアクションだと思います。

それから、みなさんのお近くに産直の販売所があれば、ぜひ訪れてみてください。こだわりを持って作られた野菜たちに「ついさっきまで、元気に大地に根を張って育っていたのかな」と想いをはせるひとときとなるでしょう。その土地の土壌や気候を活かした環境で育まれた地場の食材は、できるだけ本来の味や食感を楽しみたい、とりすぎになりやすい脂質量や塩分の量もできる限りおさえたいといった願いも叶えてくれます。収穫してから食卓に並ぶまでの時間も短く、時間が経つほどに栄養価が落ちてしまうといわれる野菜の特性にも合っています。みずみずしい野菜たちに出会ったときに、どんなふうに食べようか、何と組み合わせようか、とうれしくなるのは私だけではないはずです。

この生命力あふれる味覚を存分に楽しむ方法は、これまでのどのレシピよりも簡単。フライパンで作る蒸し野菜は、さっと火を通す程度に（37ページ参照）。グリルするときは、ひと口大に切った野菜を、ボウルであらかじめオリーブ油で表面をコーティングしてから火にかけて、野菜が本来持つ水分を閉じ込めます。仕上げに塩を少しだけ振って、甘みと香りを引き立てて。火の通りにくい野菜は、フライパン蒸しとグリルのコンビネーションがおすすめです。さらに、生でいただくサラダは、ドレッシングは使わずにそのままでまずはひと口。レタスのシャキッとしたみずみずしさの中にある甘み、ぎゅっと詰まったトマトの甘酸っぱさ、グリーンリーフの若葉ならではのやわらかさとほのかな苦み…食べるごとに口いっぱいに広がる野菜の味わいに、愛おしささえ感じることも。

大人も子どもにもこの感動を伝えていきたい、そんな思いはふくらむばかりです。

Up until now we've been looking at GOOD HABITs, simple methods and recipes that will allow you to integrate nutritional knowledge into your daily life, long term. These are all rooted in a philosophy I love; that of "food as culture".

Choosing your ingredients from a mindset of "Local production for local consumption" allows you to support your local economy, build your local culture, and bring about new forms of cultural expression. Expanded further, I believe this way of thinking is also connected to loftier goals, such as "representing Japan on the world stage," or "highlighting the food cultures of the world."

With that in mind, if you have a local market where you can buy directly from local producers, I highly suggest you check it out. It provides a great chance to think about the fact that these well-raised vegetables were growing healthily in soil until just now. Local ingredients grown in local soil receive all the benefits of their optimal environment, and allow you to enjoy their original taste and texture, meaning you don't need salt and fat to add flavor anymore. This also minimizes the time it takes each vegetable to reach your table, which is ideal considering vegetables lose their nutritional value over time. I know I'm not the only one who gets excited by the possibilities available when you find a perfectly ripe, colorful vegetable at the market.

Even better, enjoying these vibrant, fresh vegetables is easier than any other recipe. For pan-steamed vegetables, you only need to let the heat go through them a bit (see page 37). If you'd prefer to grill your vegetables, cut them into bite-size pieces, and coat in olive oil before cooking. This will help to seal in their water and flavor. Once they are done, just add a little bit of salt to bring out their sweetness and fragrance. For hard vegetables that don't hold heat well, I recommend a combination of steaming and grilling. When eating your produce raw in a salad, try taking a bite without dressing first. The sweet crunch of crisp lettuce, the acidic sweetness of a fresh tomato, the softness and subtle bitterness of young green leaves... the fresh taste of quality vegetables is something you'll fall in love with easily.

For adults and children alike, I hope you can experience for yourself the simple joy of fresh produce.

IN CONCLUSION

おわりに

良い食習慣の答えはひとつではありません。みなさんと私が同じでないように、GOOD HABITが必ずしもそれぞれのライフスタイルに合うとは限らないからです。まずはレシピからひとつを試していただいて、いつもの生活の中で「私はここをちょっと変えてみると良いのかも」といった自分の気づきの声に耳を傾けてみることです。気づいた今日が始めどき。

この本では、日本語と英語を一緒にお届けすることにこだわりました。ますます進む国際化社会の中で、「食卓がつながりの場になってほしい」という願いからです。アメリカのカンザス州に留学していたとき、英語をまったく話せなかった私にとって、ホストファミリーと一緒に料理番組を見るひとときが、今も心にあたたかく残るコミュニケーションの大切な一歩でした。きっとこれから、身近なところでも、多国籍なバックグラウンドを持つ方と知り合う機会が増えると思います。そうしたとき、この本を眺めながら一緒に料理を楽しんだり、おたがいの食文化を紹介し合ったり。みなさんと世界が楽しくつながるお手伝いができれば、これほどうれしいことはありません。

また今回、はじめての料理本の挑戦で、何から何まで手探りの制作期間でしたが、チームGOOD HABITの仲間に支えられて、自信を持ってお届けできる形になったことに感謝が尽きません。そして、ありがたい機会をいただいた山川出版社さまに心より御礼申し上げます。

私のルーツは、母の家庭料理です。小さいころから台所で母の料理をする姿を眺めるのが好きで、玉ねぎの皮むきが私の担当になったとき、とてもうれしかったのを覚えています。それからも母の作るごはんを目指して見よう見まねで続けた自己流の料理が、今こうしてみなさまに届けられる形にまでなったのは、夫がいたから。フルタイムの仕事をしながら、なんとかやりくりしていたときも、慣れない子育てに余裕がないときも、いつも一番近くで応援してくれていました。そして持ち前の豊かな発想力とユーモアで、この本の根幹を一緒に作り、何度も何度も試作品を食べてはアイデアをくれました。あなたがいたから頑張れました、本当にありがとう。

この本が多くの方のGOOD HABIT〜心はずむ毎日の、うれしい食習慣〜を始めるきっかけになること願っています。

村田 英理子

There's no single solution to dietary habits. Just like you and I are different, the GOOD HABITs that I have laid out may not perfectly fit your lifestyle. As a start, I would suggest trying out one or two of the recipes for yourself, and listening for that part of you that pushes you towards making changes for the better. Once you begin to identify the parts of your daily nutrition that you want to clean up, that's a great starting point.

For this book, I insisted on presenting most of the parts in both English and Japanese. As our society becomes more and more global, it's my sincere wish that your dinner table can become a place for people from all over the world to connect. While studying in Kansas, even though I struggled to speak English, the time spent watching cooking shows with my host family was a crucial part of our early communication. I still look back fondly on that experience. I also believe that no matter where you are reading from, you are likely to encounter more and more people from all sorts of countries. When that time comes, please use this book as one way to enjoy healthy cooking together, and discover more about each other's food cultures. Nothing in the world would make me happier than to help you come closer to your international friends and neighbors.

Truthfully, this is my first attempt at gathering my recipes into a cookbook, and there was a bit of fumbling as we put everything together. However, it's thanks to the support of my GOOD HABIT team that I can confidently present the knowledge and recipes I've gathered to all of my readers. And on the topic of gratitude, I also need to extend my sincerest thanks to Yamakawa Publishing for allowing me the opportunity to share this book with you all. I am immensely grateful to everyone involved in this project.

My roots are in my mother's home cooking. From a young age, I would love to watch my mother in the kitchen, and I still remember the excitement I had when she finally gave me my first kitchen responsibility (peeling onions). Being able to take my own style of cooking, inspired through watching my mother, and share it with all of you is only possible because of my husband. Even while I struggled to juggle managing our house while working full-time, and as I fought the uphill battle of becoming a new parent, he has always been the closest and most supportive person in my life. And with abundant creativity and humor he helped me create this book, particularly by eating prototype after prototype and helping me to discover new ideas. Tsuyoshi, it's thanks to you that I was able to come this far. Thank you from the bottom of my heart.

And lastly dear reader, thank you. I truly hope that this book will be the start of many GOOD HABITs, long-term healthy eating for a healthy life, for many people, including you and your family.

ERIKO MURATA

EDITORIAL NOTE

冬の気配が近づいてきたある日のこと。すやすや眠る小さな赤ちゃんを抱いて現れた著者は、この本に流れているのと同じ、健康的ですがすがしい空気を纏っていました。
大きな笑顔と気持ちいいほどにシンプルな思考、それと意志のある澄んだまなざしにすっかり心を打たれてはじまったGOOD HABIT。

いつだって彼女は、小さなこともゆるがせにせず、真摯に向き合ってきました。
かつては大企業の数少ない女性の総合職として、責任ある仕事と家庭との両立に励む日々を送り、それから新たな家族を迎えてもなお、心置きなく新しい挑戦を積み重ねていく。はじめての本づくりもその生き方の通り、ていねいかつ前向きな視点を授けてくれました。そこに多くのたゆまぬ努力や工夫があったことは言うまでもありません。
今の自分に合わせてしなやかに形を変えながら、好きなことを極めて活躍し続ける姿は、まさに理想。目標に向かって一歩踏み出したい、多くの人の道しるべとなるのではないでしょうか。

話を冒頭にもどすと、彼女の隣には、今日からはじまる新しい挑戦をともによろこぶ、ご主人の姿がありました。家族の幸せを願うキッチンから生まれた夢。その道のりを楽しむおふたりの、日頃からおたがいを理解し、支え合うすてきな関係にひとりの女性としても希望を感じ、自然と勇気づけられたのでした。

GOOD HABIT。良い食習慣はときに食卓をこえて、くらしを前向きにするだけでなく、自由に夢を描きながらより良く生きることにつながる。村田家の習慣が、そう教えてくれました。

この一冊にあるひとさじのアイデアが、みなさんの心豊かな毎日につながることを願って。

村田英理子 **ERIKO MURATA**

Instagram : @athlete.food_eriko.murata

むらたえりこ／兵庫県神戸市出身。幼少期にはアメリカ・ロサンゼルス在住、高校在学時にもカンザス州留学を経験。日本とアメリカに成長のルーツを持つことを生かし、兵庫県立長田高校、国際基督教大学を卒業後は国内大手鉄鋼メーカーに就職。生産管理や海外営業に従事する傍ら、元日本代表のプロラグビープレーヤー・村田毅（むらた・つよし）との結婚を機に、アスリートフードマイスターの資格を通じてスポーツ栄養の知識を習得。第1子誕生のち独立。
海外営業職とアスリートサポートを両立する中で確立した、よりシンプルに効率よく、質の高い食事を作るメソッドや、実生活に寄り添ったレシピは、運動習慣のある人だけでなく料理初心者にも好評。企業や教育機関での講演活動や、コラム執筆、など幅広く手がける。

TEAM GOOD HABIT

アートディレクション	北田進吾
デザイン	北田進吾，畠中脩大（キタダデザイン）
撮影	福尾美雪
スタイリング	久保田朋子
スタイリングアシスタント	下條絵美
イラスト	越井　隆
編集協力	久保木薫
翻訳協力	Ryan & Manami Silence
Special Thanks	片岡晴未，前島美穂，モリ洋子，平木香織

GOOD HABIT

心はずむ毎日の、うれしい食習慣

2021年1月10日　第1版第1刷印刷
2021年1月20日　第1版第1刷発行

著　者　村田英理子
発行者　野澤武史
発行所　株式会社山川出版社
〒101-0047　東京都千代田区内神田1-13-13
電話03-3293-8131（営業）　1802（編集）
https://www.yamakawa.co.jp
振替00120-9-43993

印刷・製本　アベイズム株式会社

ISBN978-4-634-15177-2 C0077